Basic English Grammar for Kids

4

Alphabet & Vowels

Write the uppercase and the lowercase letters.
(大文字と小文字を書こう!)

Uppercase (大文字) →

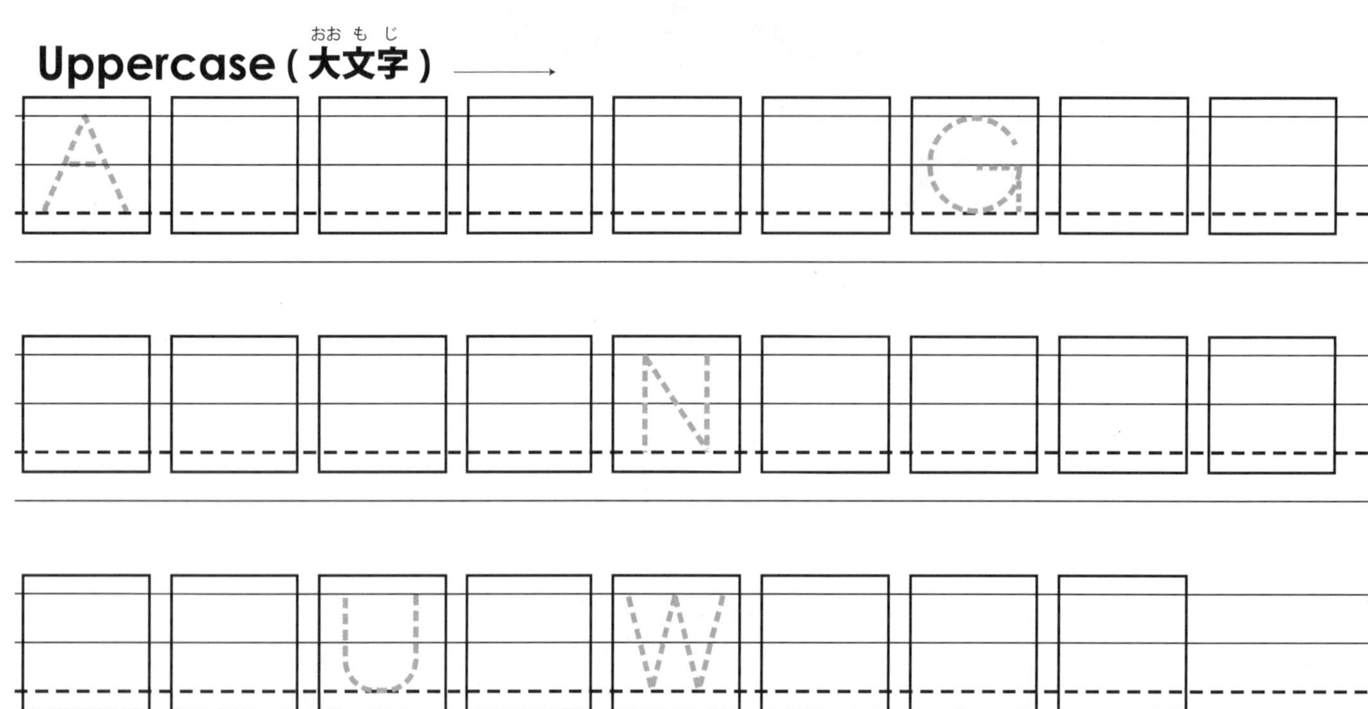

Lowercase (小文字) →

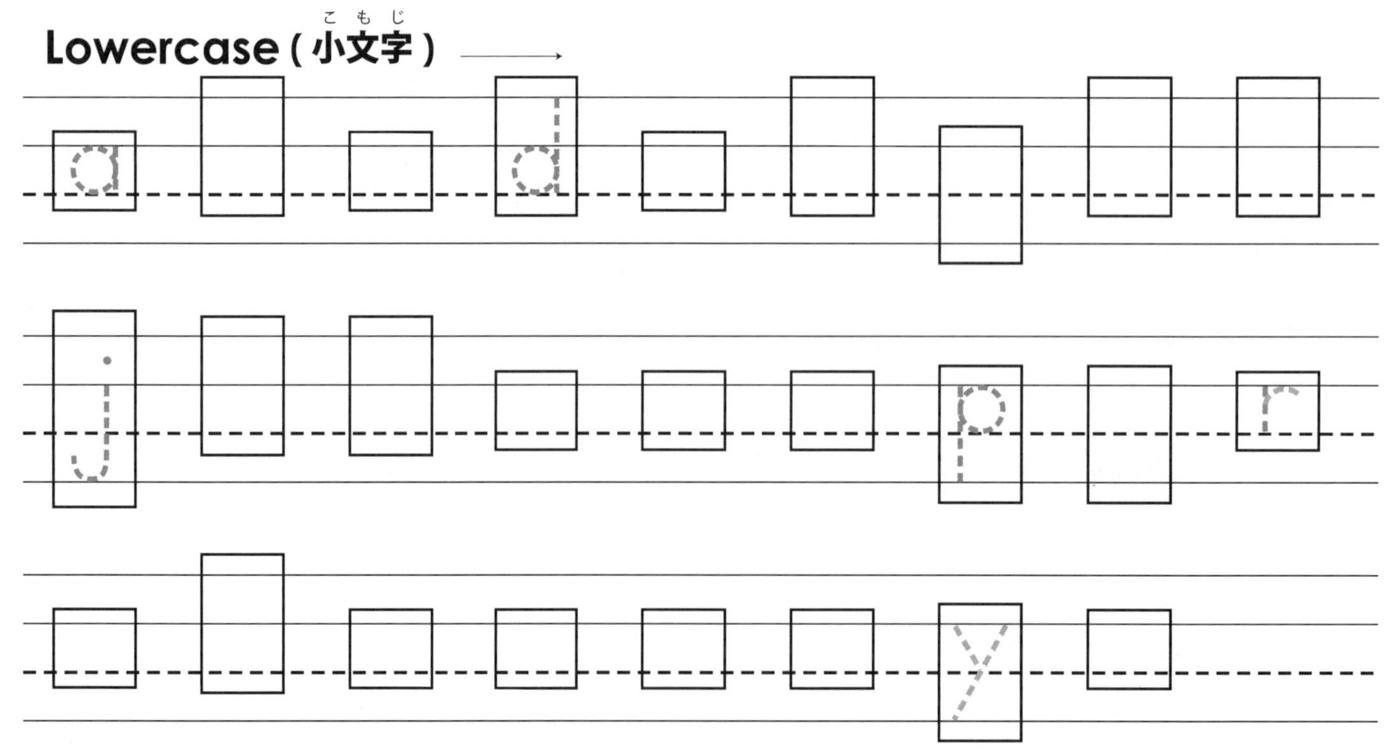

Circle the vowels below.

(お母さん文字"母音"をみつけて全部に◯をつけよう!)

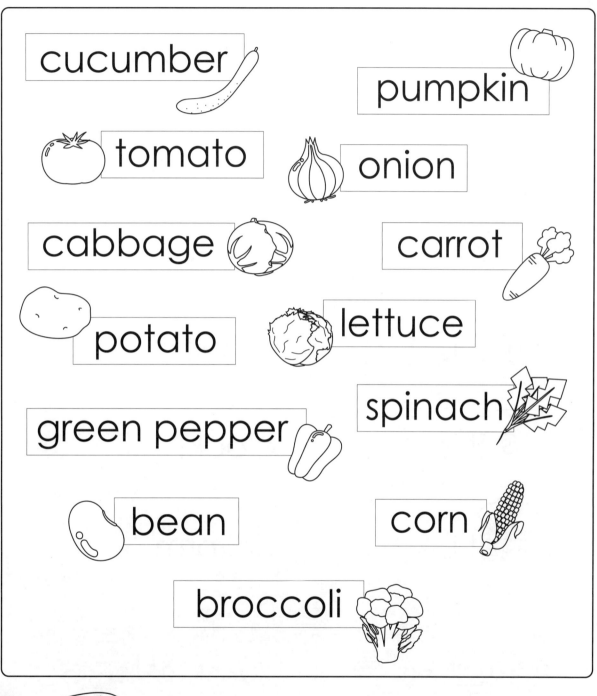

cucumber

pumpkin

tomato

onion

cabbage

carrot

potato

lettuce

spinach

green pepper

bean

corn

broccoli

Review! Write the vowels. (お母さん文字を5つ書いてみよう!)

Uppercase (大文字)					
Lowercase (小文字)					

Section 1	Grammar 1~3 Review 2	"a" vs "an"

Write "a" or "an" on the lines. (＿＿ に「a」か「an」を書こう!)

① It is ＿＿＿＿＿ elephant.

② It is ＿＿＿＿＿ peach.

音に注意! ③ It is ＿＿＿＿＿ x-ray.

④ It is ＿＿＿＿＿ orange.

⑤ It is ＿＿＿＿＿ clock.

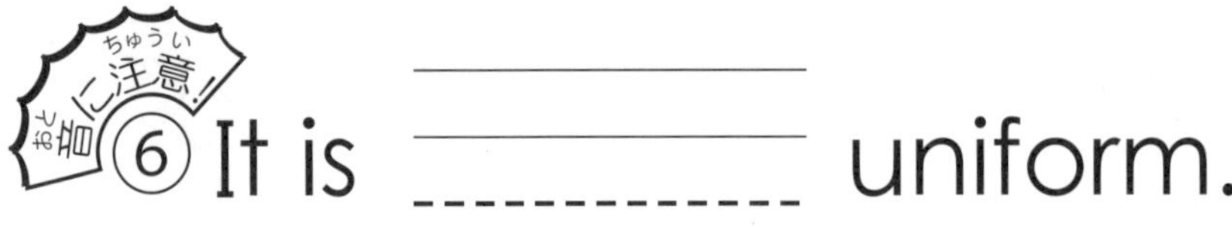

音に注意! ⑥ It is ＿＿＿＿＿ uniform.

特別なルール 世界に１つだけしかないものは数えなくてもいいよね。
だから、「a」や「an」は使わない。そのかわり「the」を使うよ！

It is ~~a~~ sun. ➡ It is **the** sun.

It is ~~a~~ moon. ➡ It is **the** moon.

It is ~~an~~ Earth. ➡ It is **the** Earth.

Write "a," "an" or "the" on the lines.

（＿＿に「a」・「an」か「the」を書こう!）

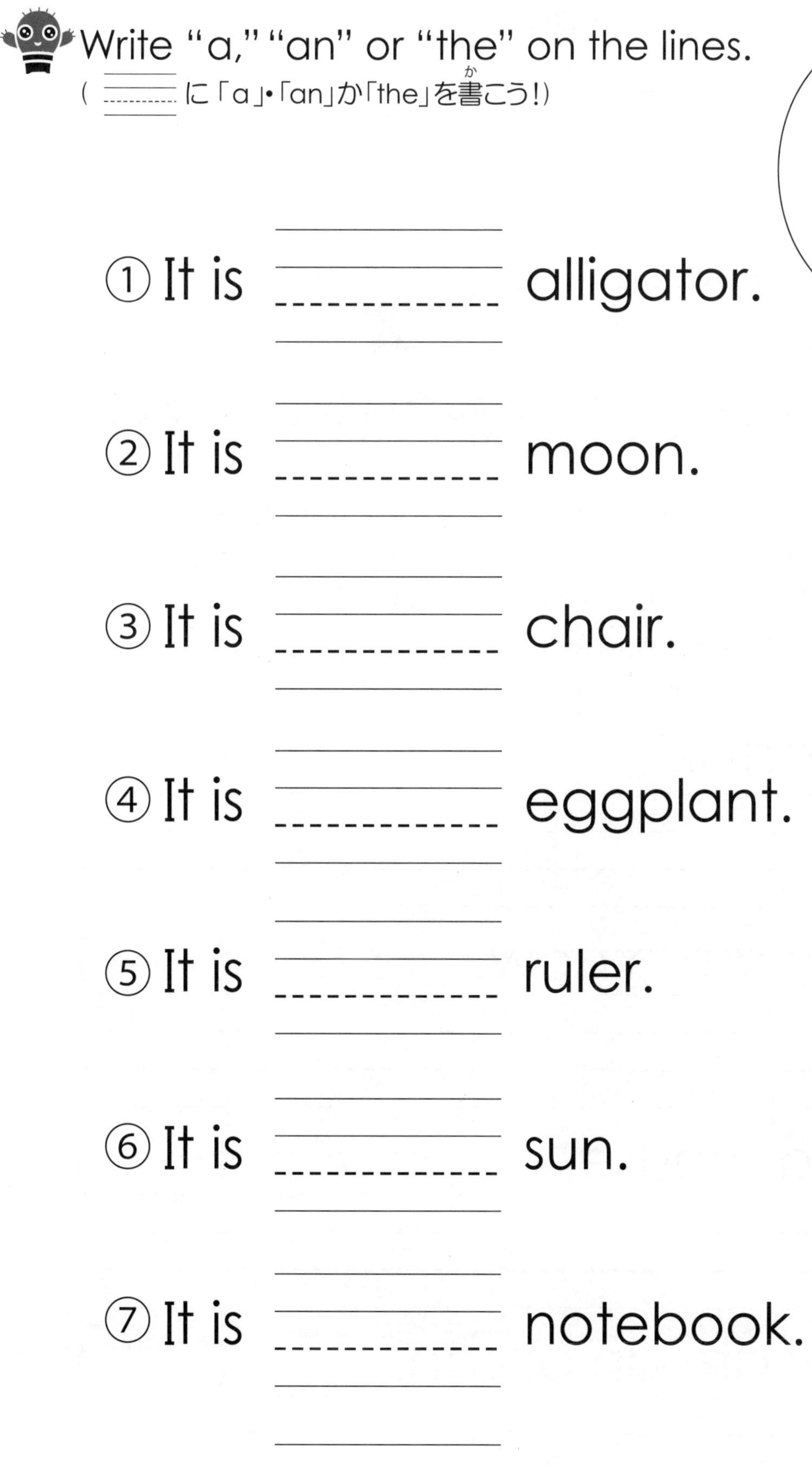

① It is ＿＿＿＿ alligator.

② It is ＿＿＿＿ moon.

③ It is ＿＿＿＿ chair.

④ It is ＿＿＿＿ eggplant.

⑤ It is ＿＿＿＿ ruler.

⑥ It is ＿＿＿＿ sun.

⑦ It is ＿＿＿＿ notebook.

⑧ It is ＿＿＿＿ Earth.

ヒント!
どんな時に
「an」や「the」を
使うのかな?

かくにん確認！

Singular vs Plural

It is（それは） ➡ 1つ/1こ　のものを表わす言葉

They are（彼らは/彼女らは/それらは）

➡ 2つ/2こ/2人以上のものを表わす言葉

だから、次の様にはならないよ！

It is apples. (✕)

They are an apple. (✕)

If the sentence is correct, put ○ in the (　　).
If the sentence is incorrect, put ✕ in the (　　).
Write the correct sentence on the lines.
（文章が正しければ○を、間違っていれば✕を(　　)に書いて、
正しい文を＿＿に書こう！）

① It is cats. (　　)

② They are a cow. (　　)

③ It is a mouse. (　　)

④ They are an apron. (　　)

⑤ They are glasses. (　　)

Write "It is" or "They are" on the lines.

（＿＿に「It is」か「They are」を書こう!）

① ＿＿＿＿＿＿＿＿ glasses.

② ＿＿＿＿＿＿＿＿ an oven.

③ ＿＿＿＿＿＿＿＿ pants.

④ ＿＿＿＿＿＿＿＿ a plate.

⑤ ＿＿＿＿＿＿＿＿ the moon.

⑥ ＿＿＿＿＿＿＿＿ an umbrella.

⑦ ＿＿＿＿＿＿＿＿ the sun.

⑧ ＿＿＿＿＿＿＿＿ shoes.

Choose the correct word and write it on the lines.
(正しい言葉を下から選んで ______ の上に書こう!)

① They are ______________________.

② It is a ______________________.

③ They are ______________________.

④ It is an ______________________.

⑤ They are ______________________.

⑥ It is a ______________________.

⑦ They are ______________________.

⑧ It is a ______________________.

gloves / glove / potatoes / potato
onions / onion / socks / sock

Rearrange the words to make a sentence.

(( )の言葉を並べかえて＿＿に正しい文を作ろう!)

文のはじめの文字は大文字になるよ！

①(is / it / . / acorn / an)

②(trees / are / . / they)

③(they / . / grapes / are)

④(it / sun / the / . / is)

⑤(are / they / pants / .)

⑥(mouse / . / it / a / is)

⑦(an / ostrich / is / . / it)

⑧(it / the / moon / is / .)

Write the Japanese in the (　　).

(次の言葉の意味を(　)に日本語で書こう!)

I (　　　　　　) We (　　　　　　)

You (　　　　　　) You (　　　　　　)

He (　　　　　　) They (　　　　　　)

She (　　　　　　)

It (　　　　　　)

Connect the pronouns and *be* verbs below.

(代名詞と*be*動詞の am / is / are を線で結ぼう!)

Pronouns	*be* verbs
I •	
You •	
He •	• am
She •	
It •	• is
We •	
You •	• are
They •	

Write the correct *be* verbs and read the sentences.
(文を読んでみよう！その後で ＿＿ に正しい「*be* 動詞」を書こう！)

【例】

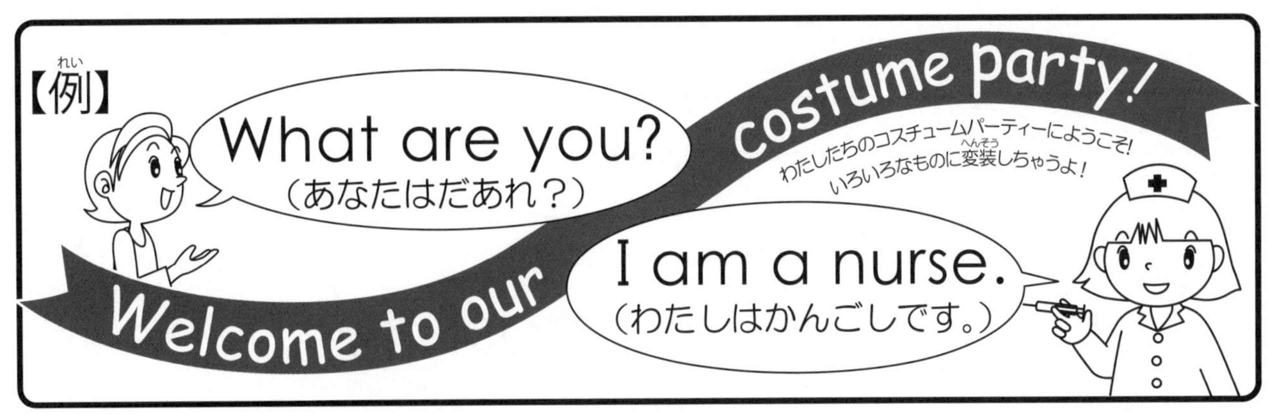
What are you?
（あなたはだあれ？）
costume party!
わたしたちのコスチュームパーティーにようこそ!
いろいろなものに変装しちゃうよ!
I am a nurse.
（わたしはかんごしです。）
Welcome to our

①

What ＿＿ you?

I ＿＿ a doctor.

②

What ＿＿ you?

I ＿＿ a pilot.

③

What ＿＿ you?

We ＿＿ bakers.

④

What ＿＿ it?

It ＿＿ a jellyfish.

Write the correct *be* verbs and read the sentences.

(文を読んでみよう！その後で ＿＿ に正しい「*be* 動詞」を書こう！)

ヒント！
「am」「is」「are」のどれかな？

① What ＿＿ you?
I ＿＿ a ghost.

② What ＿＿ she?
She ＿＿ a witch.

③ What ＿＿ it?
It ＿＿ a skeleton.

④ What ＿＿ they?
They ＿＿ bats.

⑤ What ＿＿ you?
We ＿＿ students.

You are a boy. ➡ Are you a boy?

「代名詞(だいめいし)」と「*be*動詞(どうし)」は、場所(ばしょ)を交換(こうかん)すると質問(しつもん)する文(ぶん)になるんだね！

Write the correct *be* verbs on the lines.
（＿＿＿に正(ただ)しい「be動詞(どうし)」を書(か)こう！）

文(ぶん)のはじめの文字(もじ)は大文字(おおもじ)になるよ！

①I ＿＿＿ a girl. ➡ ＿＿＿ I a girl?

②You ＿＿＿ a doctor. ➡ ＿＿＿ you a doctor?

③He ＿＿＿ a pianist. ➡ ＿＿＿ he a pianist?

④She ＿＿＿ a dentist. ➡ ＿＿＿ she a dentist?

⑤It ＿＿＿ an insect. ➡ ＿＿＿ it an insect?

⑥We ＿＿＿ scientists. ➡ ＿＿＿ we scientists?

⑦You ＿＿＿ astronauts.
➡ ＿＿＿ you astronauts?

⑧They ＿＿＿ animals. ➡ ＿＿＿ they animals?

① I am a Japanese student.

（わたしは日本人学生です。）

（わたしは日本人学生ですか？）

② You are an American student.

（あなたはアメリカ人学生です。）

⇨ ＿＿ ＿＿ an American student?

（あなたはアメリカ人学生ですか？）

③ He is a Chinese student.

（かれは中国人学生です。）

⇨ ＿＿ ＿＿ a Chinese student?

（かれは中国人学生ですか？）

④ She is a Korean student.

（かのじょは韓国人学生です。）

⇨ ＿＿ ＿＿ a Korean student?

（かのじょは韓国人学生ですか？）

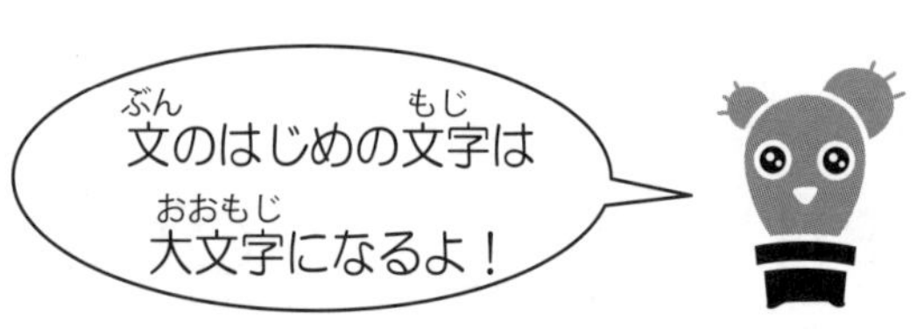

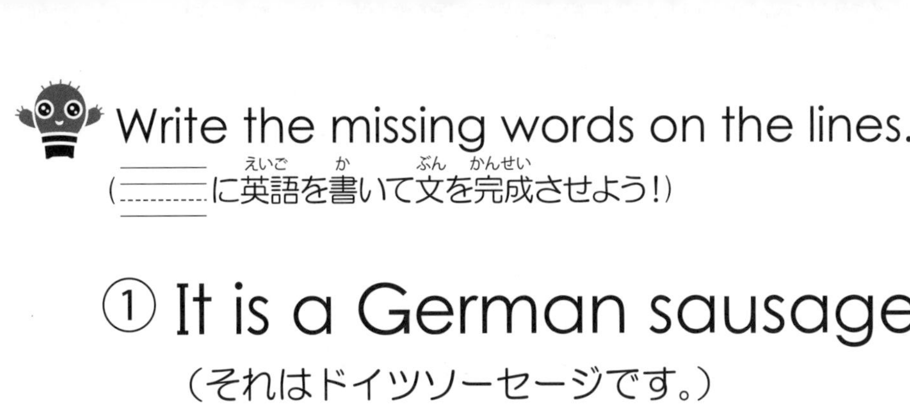

Write the missing words on the lines.
（______に英語を書いて文を完成させよう！）

① It is a German sausage.
（それはドイツソーセージです。）

⇨ ______ ______ a German sausage?
（それはドイツソーセージですか？）

② We are Canadian students.
（わたしたちはカナダ人学生です。）

⇨ ______ ______ Canadian students?
（わたしたちはカナダ人学生ですか？）

③ You are Indian students.
（あなたたちはインド人学生です。）

⇨ ______ ______ Indian students?
（あなたたちはインド人学生ですか？）

④ They are British students.
（かれらはイギリス人学生です。）

⇨ ______ ______ British students?
（かれらはイギリス人学生ですか？）

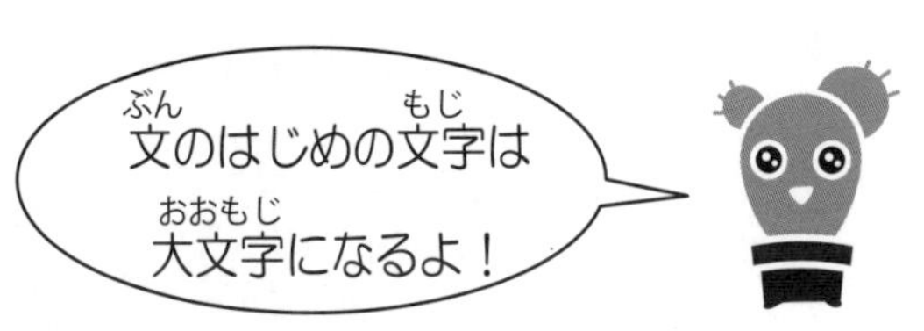

Write the correct *be* verbs on the lines.

（＿＿に正しい「*be*動詞」を書こう！）

① ＿＿ he a police officer?
Yes, he ＿＿.
② ＿＿ you a scientist?
No, I ＿＿ not.
③ ＿＿ she a pianist?
No, she ＿＿ not.
④ ＿＿ it a riceball?
Yes, it ＿＿.
⑤ ＿＿ they bakers?
Yes, they ＿＿.
文のはじめの文字は
大文字になるよ！

Write the correct *be* verbs on the lines.
（＿＿に正しい「*be*動詞」を書こう！）

① ＿＿＿ we dancers?

Yes, you ＿＿＿.

② ＿＿＿ I a fisherman?

No, you ＿＿＿ not.

③ ＿＿＿ you office workers?

Yes, we ＿＿＿.

④ ＿＿＿ it a grasshopper?

No, it ＿＿＿ not.

⑤ ＿＿＿ she a waitress?

Yes, she ＿＿＿.

文のはじめの文字は大文字になるよ！

Rearrange the words to make a sentence.

((　)の言葉を並べかえて＿＿に正しい文を作ろう!)

文のはじめの文字は大文字になるよ！

① (am / a / I / teacher / .)

② (? / you / are / a / farmer)

③ (he / is / student / a / ?)

④ (is / actress / she / an / .)

⑤ (it / mouse / a / is / ?)

⑥ (scientists / . / are / we)

⑦ (they / teachers / ? / are)

⑧ (are / you / ? / artists)

物のようすを表わす言葉（形容詞）が後ろにくることもあるよ！

例 I am tall.（ぼくは背が高い）

They are young.（かれらは若い）

この時は I am ~~a~~ tall. や They are young~~s~~. にはならない！

「tall」や「young」は物ではないから数えられないよ。気をつけてね!!

Rearrange the words to make a sentence.

（（　）の言葉を並べかえて＿＿に正しい文を作ろう！）

文のはじめの文字は大文字になるよ！

①（ are / we / cold / ? ）

②（ windy / is / it / . ）

③（ she / happy / is / . ）

④（ old / are / they / ? ）

⑤（ hungry / I / am / . ）

⑥（ is / he / full / ? ）

Follow the maze to find out how to spell the words. Write the words in the spaces below.

(迷路(めいろ)をやって動作(どうさ)を表(あらわ)す言葉(ことば)を見(み)つけよう。見(み)つけた順(じゅん)に下(した)に書(か)いてみよう!)

Start →

c u t l f y n u r g o r y c ↓ ↑ ← ← → ↓

Finish

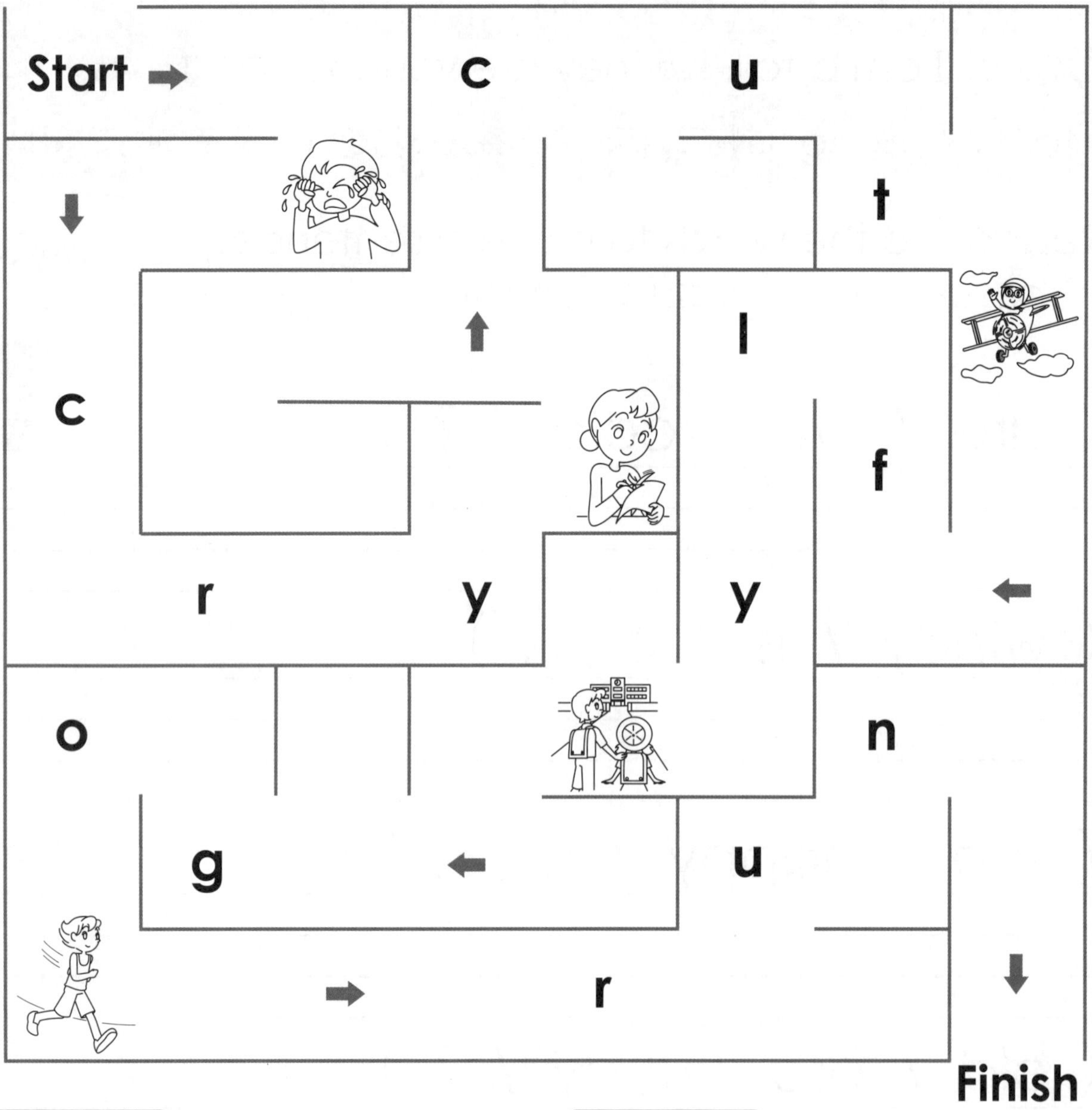

Fill in the words in the grid to find the hidden word.
Then write the hidden word to complete the word list.
(右のヒントを参考に左の表に当てはまる言葉を選んで□に1文字づつ書こう!)

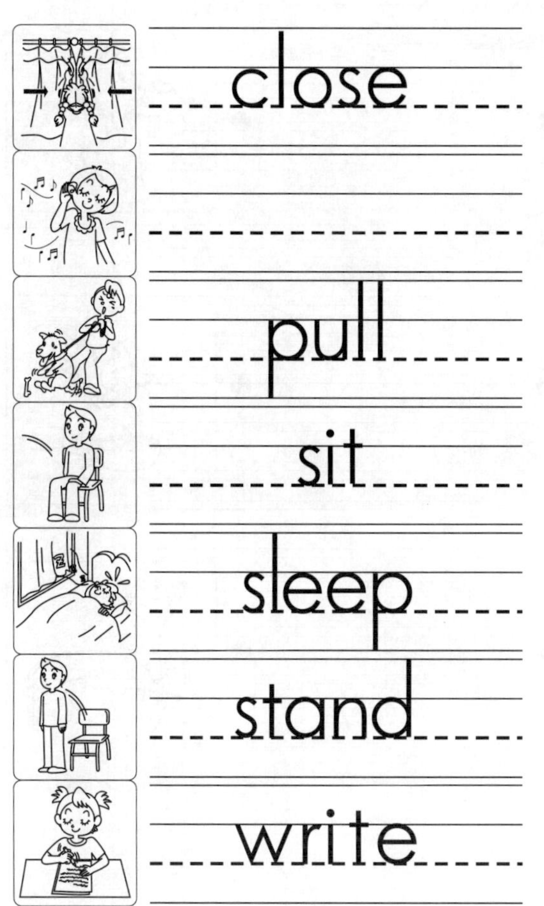

Write these words forward. Then connect the words to the pictures.
(左の言葉を正しい形で書こう！ 書いたら右の絵で合うものと線でつなごう！)

① eat

② drink

③ jump

④ like

⑤ play

⑥ swim

Can you find all the words in the word worm?

(次の中から下の全ての言葉を探せるかな？)

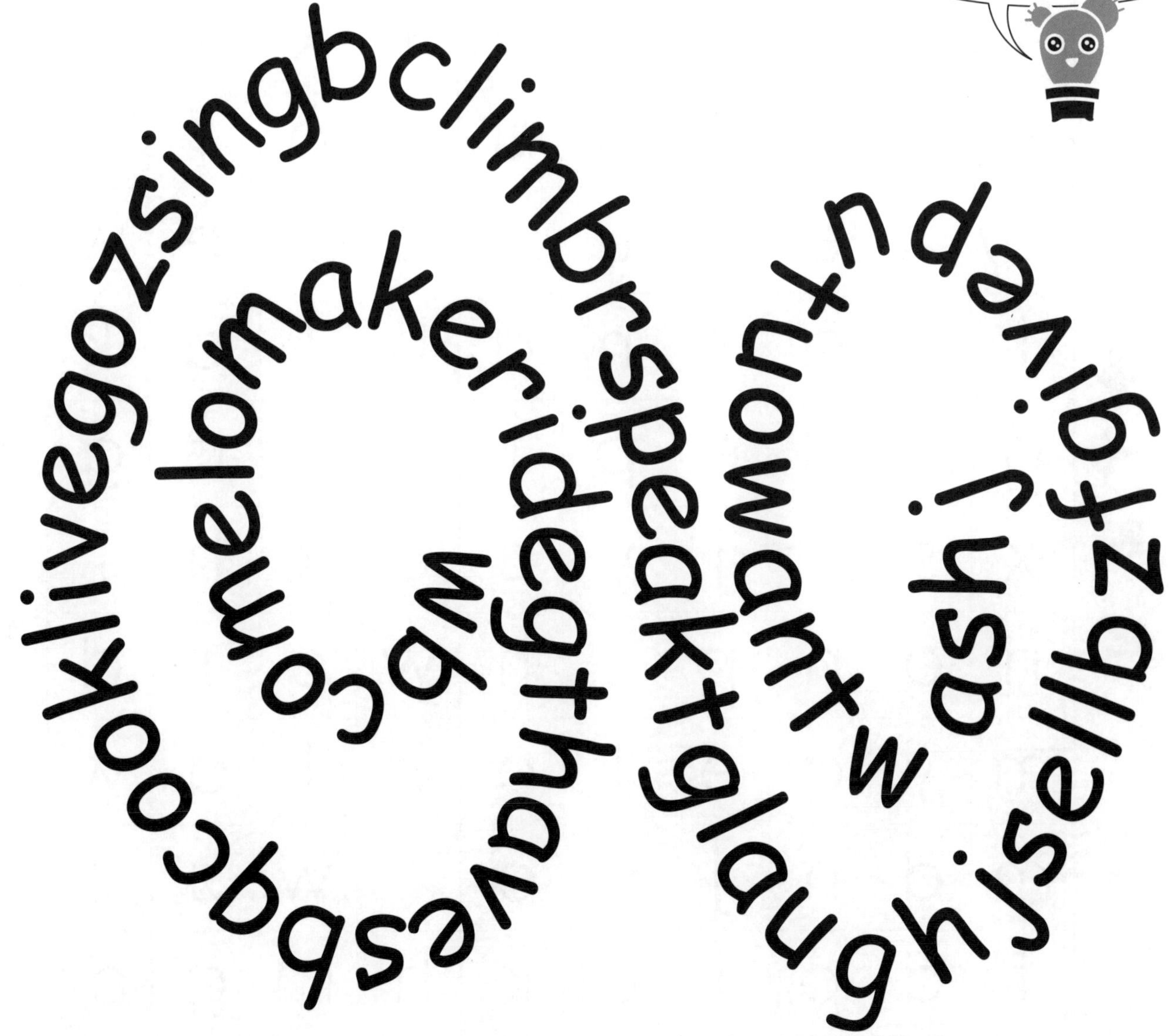

見つけたら〇でかこもう！

comelomakeridegthavesbqcooklivegozsingbclimbrspeaktglaughjsellbzgfgiveputuowantwashj

 climb

 come

 cook

 give

 have

laugh

 live

 make

 put

 ride

 sell

 sing

speak

 want

 wash

Can you find all the words in the grid below?

(次の中から下の全ての言葉を探せるかな？)

t	r	s	p	y	y	f	k	s	d
e	e	r	t	u	u	q	o	t	k
g	r	e	x	u	s	b	o	e	w
l	e	a	r	n	d	h	l	a	k
o	x	d	e	p	t	y	t	c	g
x	s	v	j	y	p	c	t	h	l
n	o	n	p	s	h	w	a	r	d
m	y	a	e	l	o	k	l	a	w
m	d	n	j	q	e	z	w	z	c
f	d	p	i	c	k	h	m	g	d

buy

help

move

read

teach

draw

learn

pick

send

walk

~~get~~

look

push

study

watch

Can you find all the words?

(次の中から下の全ての言葉を書けるかな？)

(Crossword grid, numbered 1–22)

Across →

Down ↓

Connect the words below. (英語(えいご)と日本語(にほんご)を線(せん)で結(むす)ぼう!)

English	日本語
catch	料理(りょうり)する
close	閉(し)める
cook	つかまえる
cut	食(た)べる
drink	行(い)く
eat	飲(の)む
go	切(き)る
open	引(ひ)く
pull	開(あ)ける

Connect the words below. （英語と日本語を線で結ぼう！）

push	歌う
run	立つ
sing	ねむる
sit	走る
sleep	なげる
stand	押す
swim	歩く
throw	座る
walk	泳ぐ

Connect the words below. (英語と日本語を線で結ぼう!)

climb •	• 飛ぶ
draw •	• 好き
fly •	• 登る
have •	• 描く
jump •	• ジャンプする
like •	• 持つ
listen •	• 作る
look •	• 聞く
make •	• 見る

Connect the words below. (英語(えいご)と日本語(にほんご)を線(せん)で結(むす)ぼう!)

pick	置(お)く
play	勉強(べんきょう)する
put	取(と)る
read	遊(あそ)ぶ
ride	さわる
study	乗(の)る
touch	読(よ)む
wash	書(か)く
write	洗(あら)う

Connect the words below. (英語(えいご)と日本語(にほんご)を線(せん)で結(むす)ぼう!)

English		Japanese
buy		泣(な)く
come		買(か)う
cry		笑(わら)う
get		もらう
give		習(なら)う
hear		来(く)る
help		聞(き)く/聞(き)こえる
laugh		あげる
learn		助(たす)ける

Connect the words below. (英語(えいご)と日本語(にほんご)を線(せん)で結(むす)ぼう!)

live	売(う)る
move	動(うご)く
sell	送(おく)る
send	使(つか)う
speak	欲(ほ)しい
teach	教(おし)える
use	見(み)る
want	住(す)む
watch	話(はな)す

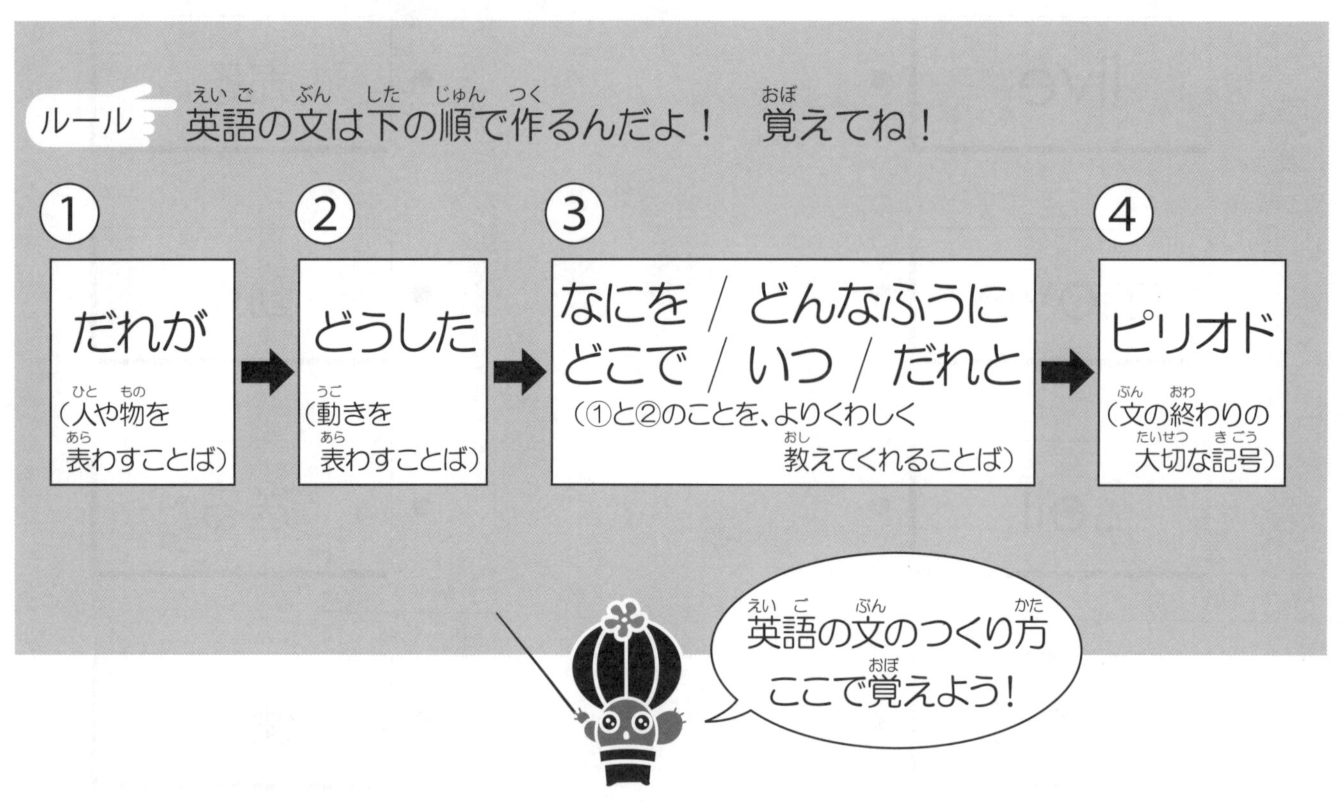
ルール 英語の文は下の順で作るんだよ！ 覚えてね！
① だれが （人や物を表わすことば）
② どうした （動きを表わすことば）
③ なにを / どんなふうに どこで / いつ / だれと （①と②のことを、よりくわしく教えてくれることば）
④ ピリオド （文の終わりの大切な記号）
英語の文のつくり方 ここで覚えよう！

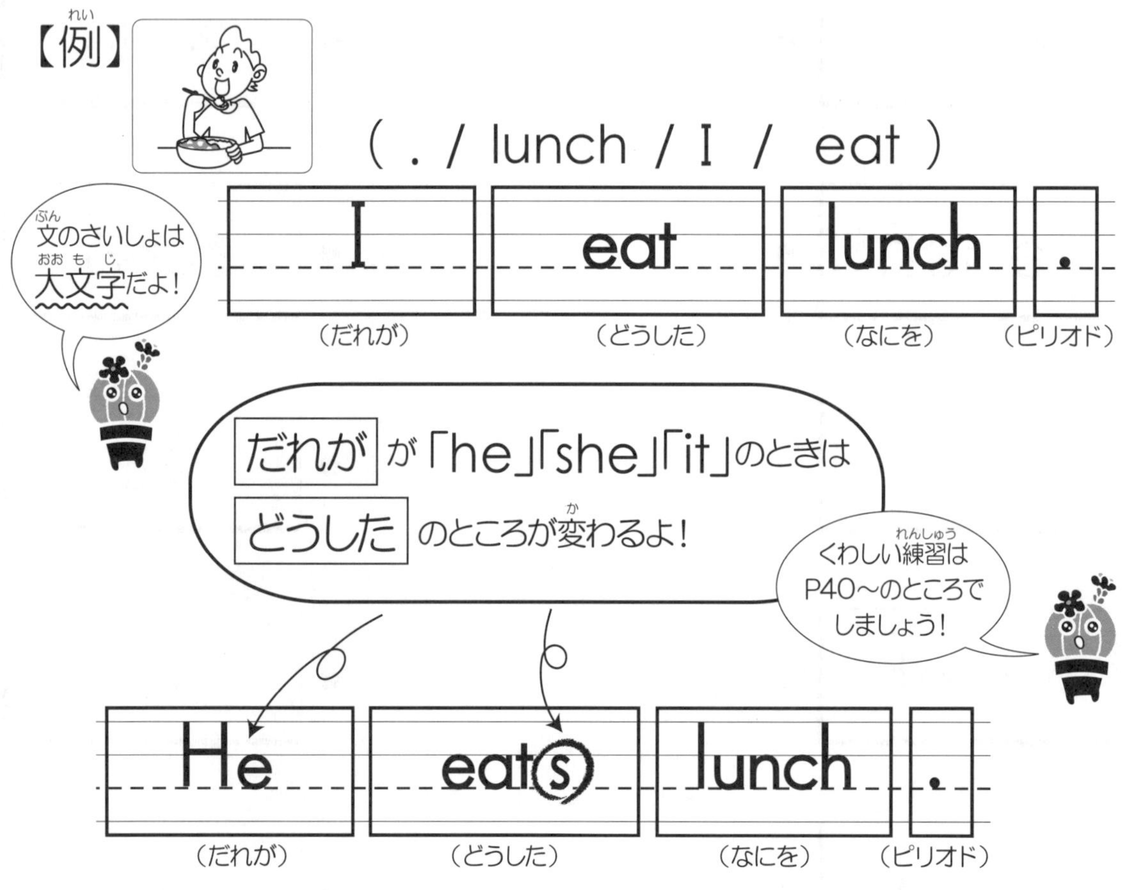
【例】
(. / lunch / I / eat)
文のさいしょは大文字だよ！
I eat lunch .
（だれが） （どうした） （なにを） （ピリオド）
だれが が「he」「she」「it」のときは どうした のところが変わるよ！
くわしい練習はP40～のところでしましょう！
He eats lunch .
（だれが） （どうした） （なにを） （ピリオド）

Rearrange the words to make a sentence.

(次の英語を正しく並べかえて、絵に合う英語の文を作ろう!)

だれが が「he」「she」「it」のときは どうした のところの「~s, ~es」に注目しよう!!

① (watches / . / TV / She)

(だれが) (どうした) (なにを)

② (birds / . / You / hear)

(だれが) (どうした) (なにを)

③ (He / in Japan / . / lives)

(だれが) (どうした) (どこに)

④ (I / English / teach / .)

(だれが) (どうした) (なにを)

⑤ (buys / . / He / bananas)

(だれが) (どうした) (なにを)

Rearrange the words to make a sentence.

(次の英語を正しく並べかえて、絵に合う英語の文を作ろう！)

だれが が「he」「she」「it」のときは どうした のところの「~s, ~es」に注目しよう!!

① (come / . / to school / We)

(だれが) (どうした) (どこへ)

② (every day / . / cry / You)

(だれが) (どうした) (いつ)

③ (a present / She / gets / .)

(だれが) (どうした) (なにを)

④ (wants / . / She / a dress)

(だれが) (どうした) (なにを)

⑤ (my mother / . / help / I)

(だれが) (どうした) (だれを)

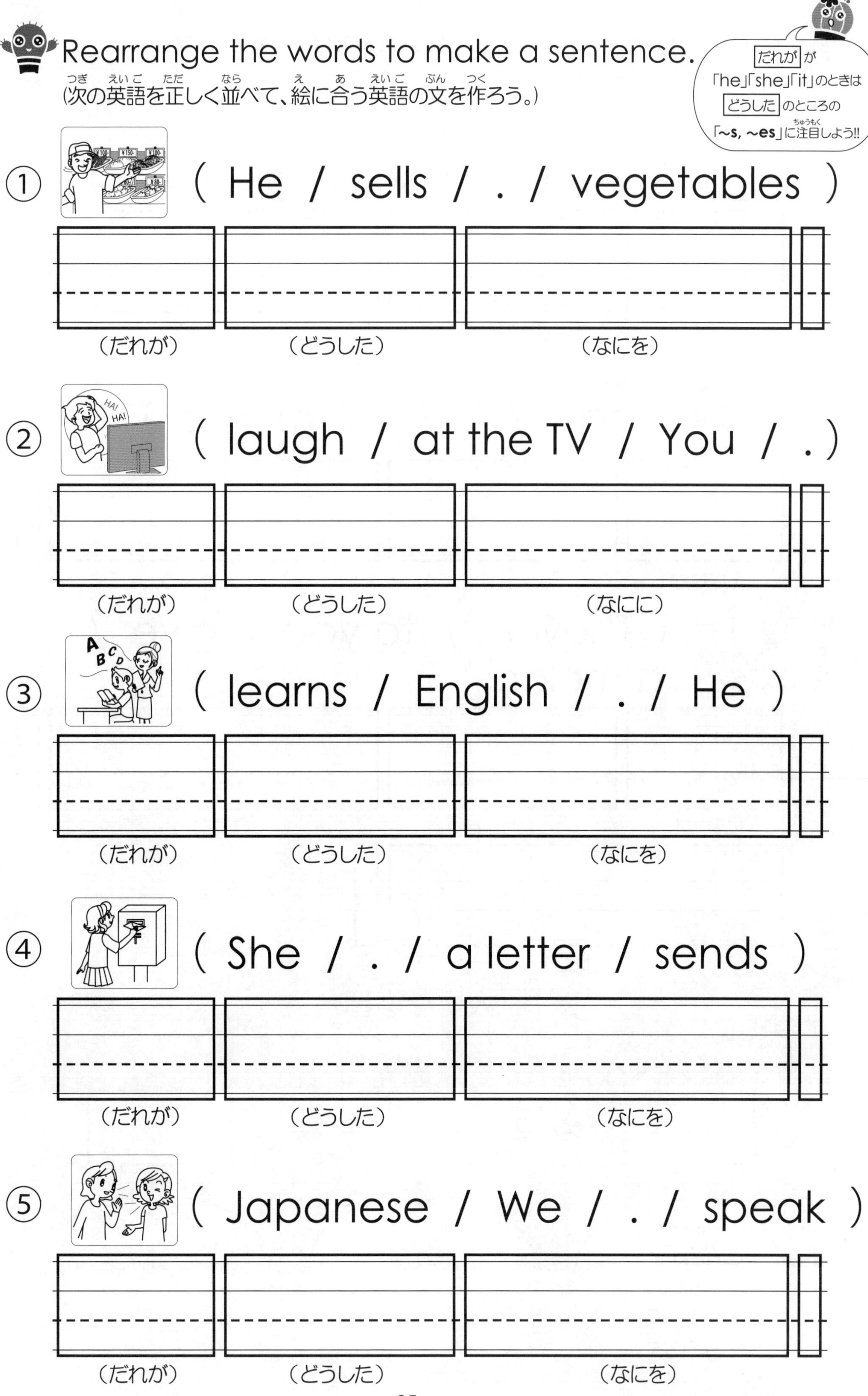

Rearrange the words to make a sentence.

(次の英語を正しく並べて、絵に合う英語の文を作ろう。)

だれが が「he」「she」「it」のときは どうした のところの「~s, ~es」に注目しよう!!

① (He / sells / . / vegetables)

(だれが) (どうした) (なにを)

② (laugh / at the TV / You / .)

(だれが) (どうした) (なにに)

③ (learns / English / . / He)

(だれが) (どうした) (なにを)

④ (She / . / a letter / sends)

(だれが) (どうした) (なにを)

⑤ (Japanese / We / . / speak)

(だれが) (どうした) (なにを)

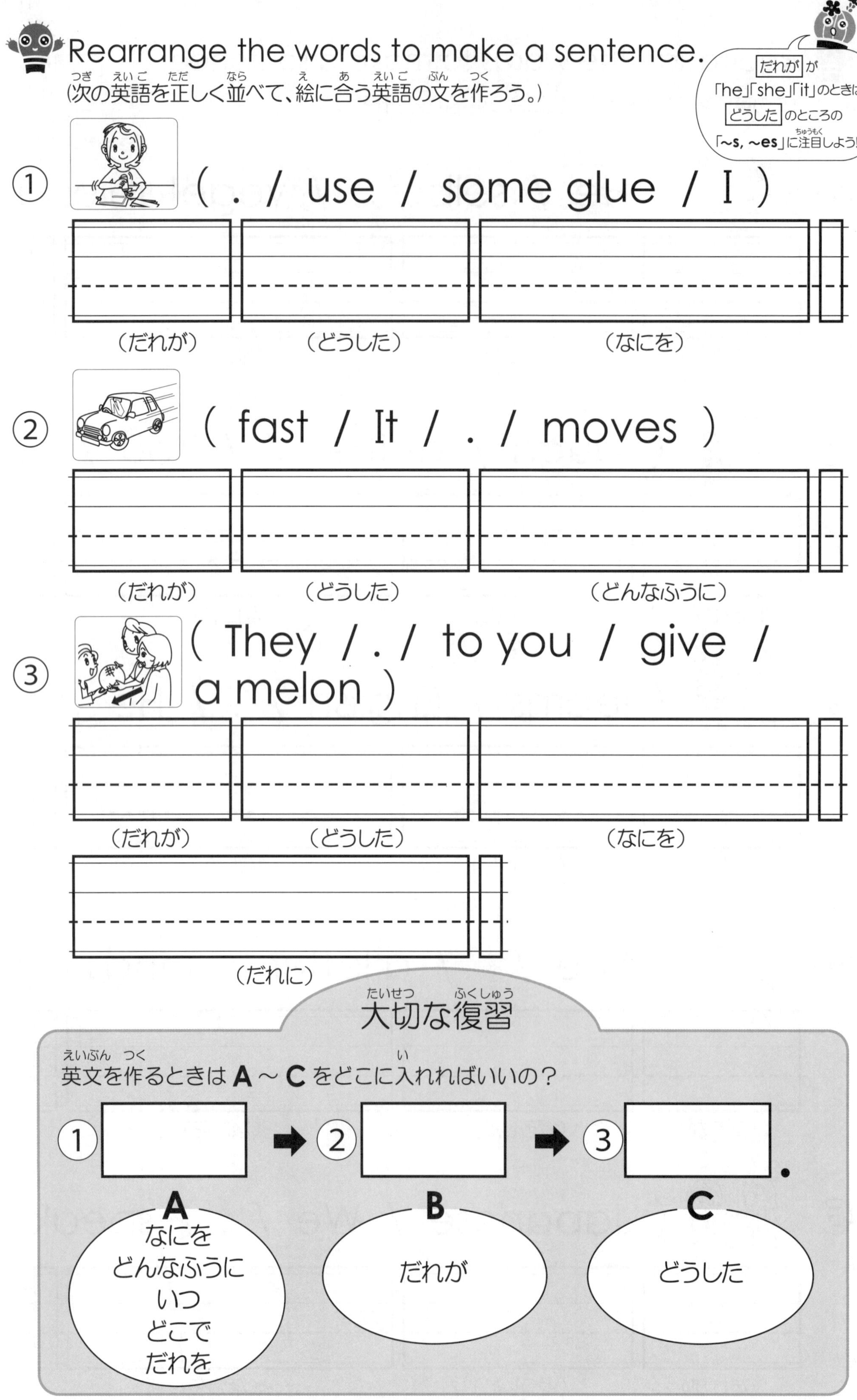

Rearrange the words to make a sentence.

(次の英語を正しく並べて、絵に合う英語の文を作ろう。)

① (. / use / some glue / I)

(だれが)　(どうした)　(なにを)

② (fast / It / . / moves)

(だれが)　(どうした)　(どんなふうに)

③ (They / . / to you / give / a melon)

(だれが)　(どうした)　(なにを)

(だれに)

大切な復習

英文を作るときは **A** ~ **C** をどこに入れればいいの?

① □ ➡ ② □ ➡ ③ □ .

A
なにを
どんなふうに
いつ
どこで
だれを

B
だれが

C
どうした

Rearrange the words to make a sentence.

(次の英語を正しく並べて、絵に合う英語の文を作ろう。)

だれが が「he」「she」「it」のときは どうした のところの「~s, ~es」に注目しよう!!

①

(だれが) (どうした) (なにを)

②

(だれが) (どうした) (どこで)

③

(だれが) (どうした) (なにを)

④

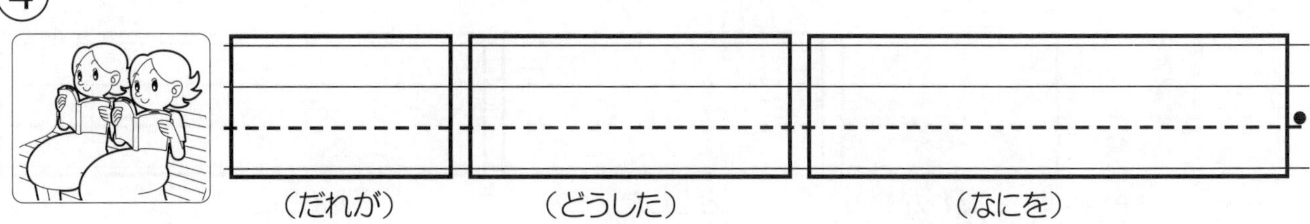

(だれが) (どうした) (なにを)

I	read	the cheese
She	makes	books
It	eats	in the pool
They	swim	a dress

Rearrange the words to make a sentence.

(次の英語を正しく並べて、絵に合う英語の文を作ろう。)

だれが が
「he」「she」「it」のときは
どうした のところの
「~s, ~es」に注目しよう!!

①

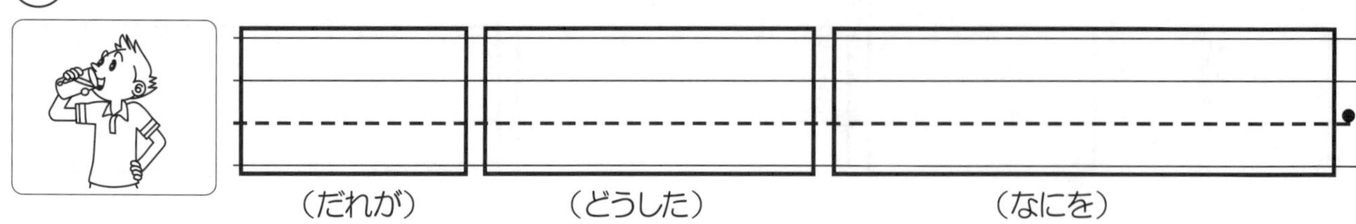

②

③

④

He	play	English
We	walk	water
I	drinks	soccer
She	learns	to school

Rearrange the words to make a sentence.

(次の英語を正しく並べて、絵に合う英語の文を作ろう。)

だれがが
「he」「she」「it」のときは
どうしたのところの
「**~s, ~es**」に注目しよう!!

①

②

③

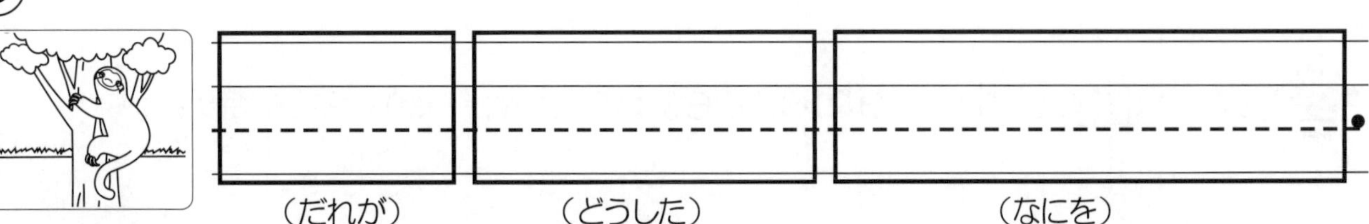

④

I	open	to music
He	listen	the box
It	climbs	math
They	studies	the tree

Section 1	Grammar 1~3 Review 6	Present Tense Conjugation

 Let's read the sentences below. (次の文を読んでみよう！)

I like strawberries.

You like potatoes.

He like**s** tomatoes.

She like**s** bananas.

It like**s** carrots.

We like peaches.

You like onions.

They like grapes.

【例】

I run fast.

（わたしは速く走ります）

He runs fast.

（彼は速く走ります）

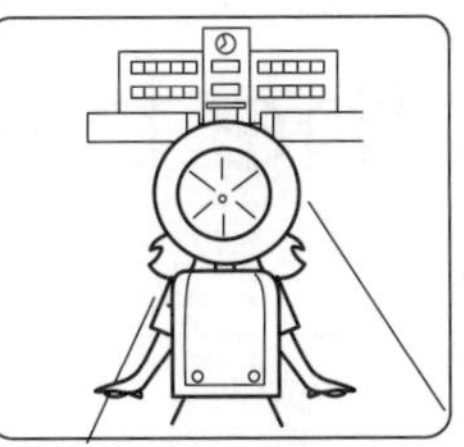

I go to school.

（わたしは学校に行きます）

She goes to school.

（彼女は学校に行きます）

fly

I fly in the garden.

（わたしは庭を飛びます）

It flies in the garden.

（それは庭を飛びます）

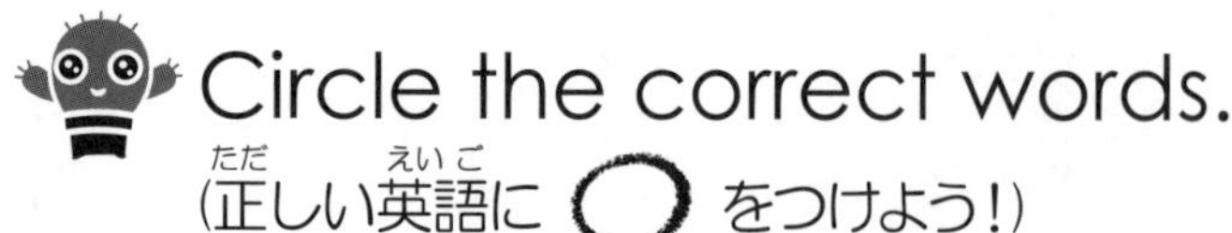

Circle the correct words.
（正しい英語に ◯ をつけよう！）

① 

She (wash / washes) the dog.

② 

He (cook / cooks) dinner.

③ 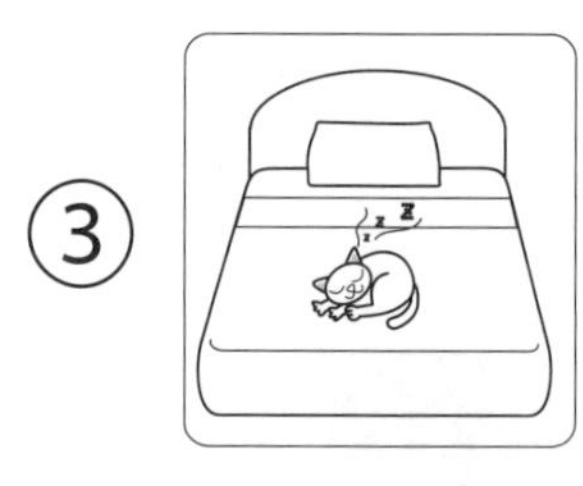

It (sleep / sleeps) on the bed.

④ 

We (watch / watches) TV every day.

⑤ 

She (teach / teaches) every day.

⑥ 

He (study / studies) English.

⑦ 

I (give / gives) you an apple.

Circle the correct words.

（正しい英語に ◯ をつけよう！）

①  I (read / reads) a book.

② 

They (speak / speaks) every day.

③  He (run / runs) every day.

④  They (play / plays) soccer.

⑤  It (fly / flies) in the garden.

⑥  I (drink / drinks) juice.

⑦  She (want / wants) a dress.

Mark correct sentences with ◯.
Mark incorrect ones with ✕ and correct the verb.

(下の文を読んで正しい時は◯、間違っている時は✕を（　）に入れ［　　］に正しい英語を書きましょう。)

【例】

あれれ？ s や es がない文があるよ！

She like monkeys. （✕）
→ likes

① It climb the tree. （　　）
→ [　　　　]

② She closes the curtains. （　　）
→ [　　　　]

③ I swim fast. （　　）
→ [　　　　]

④ We buys some food. （　　）
→ [　　　　]

⑤ She want a dress. （　　）
→ [　　　　]

s や es がいらない文があるよ！

Mark correct sentences with ◯.
Mark incorrect ones with ✕ and correct the verb.
(下の文を読んで正しい時は◯、間違っている時は✕を(　)に入れ［　　］に正しい英語を書きましょう。)

あれれ？
s や es がない文があるよ！

① I gets a present. (　　)
→ ［　　　　］

② We go to school. (　　)
→ ［　　　　］

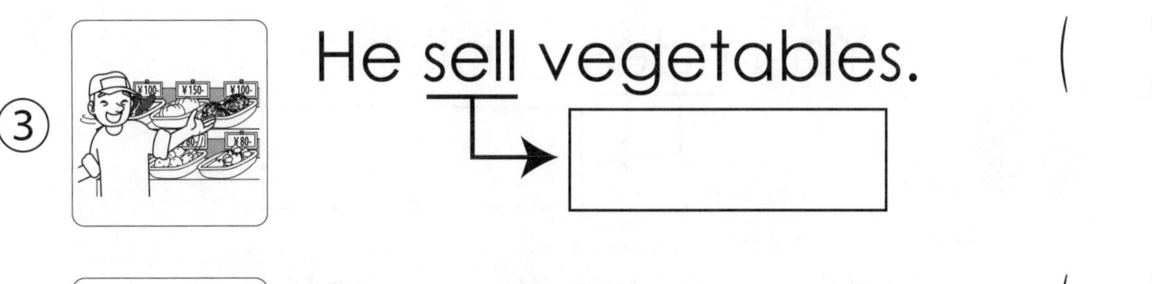

③ He sell vegetables. (　　)
→ ［　　　　］

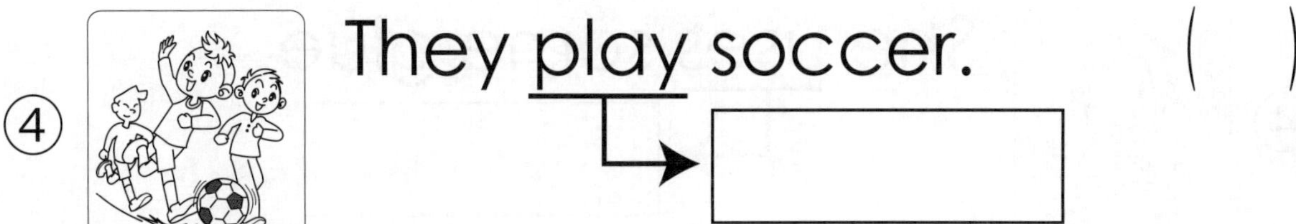

④ They play soccer. (　　)
→ ［　　　　］

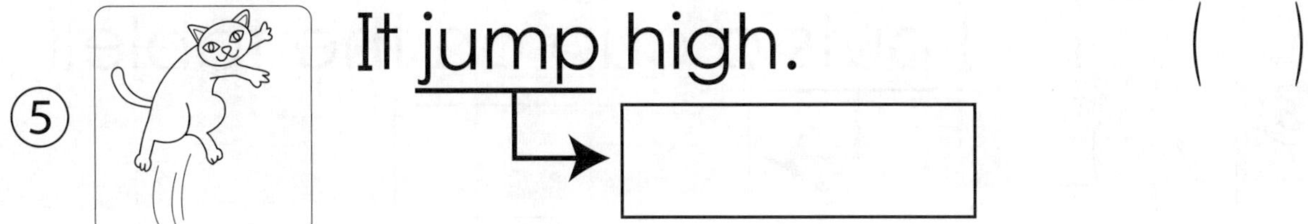

⑤ It jump high. (　　)
→ ［　　　　］

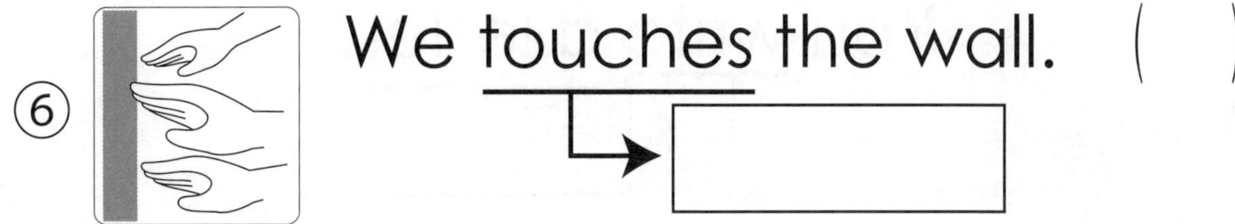

⑥ We touches the wall. (　　)
→ ［　　　　］

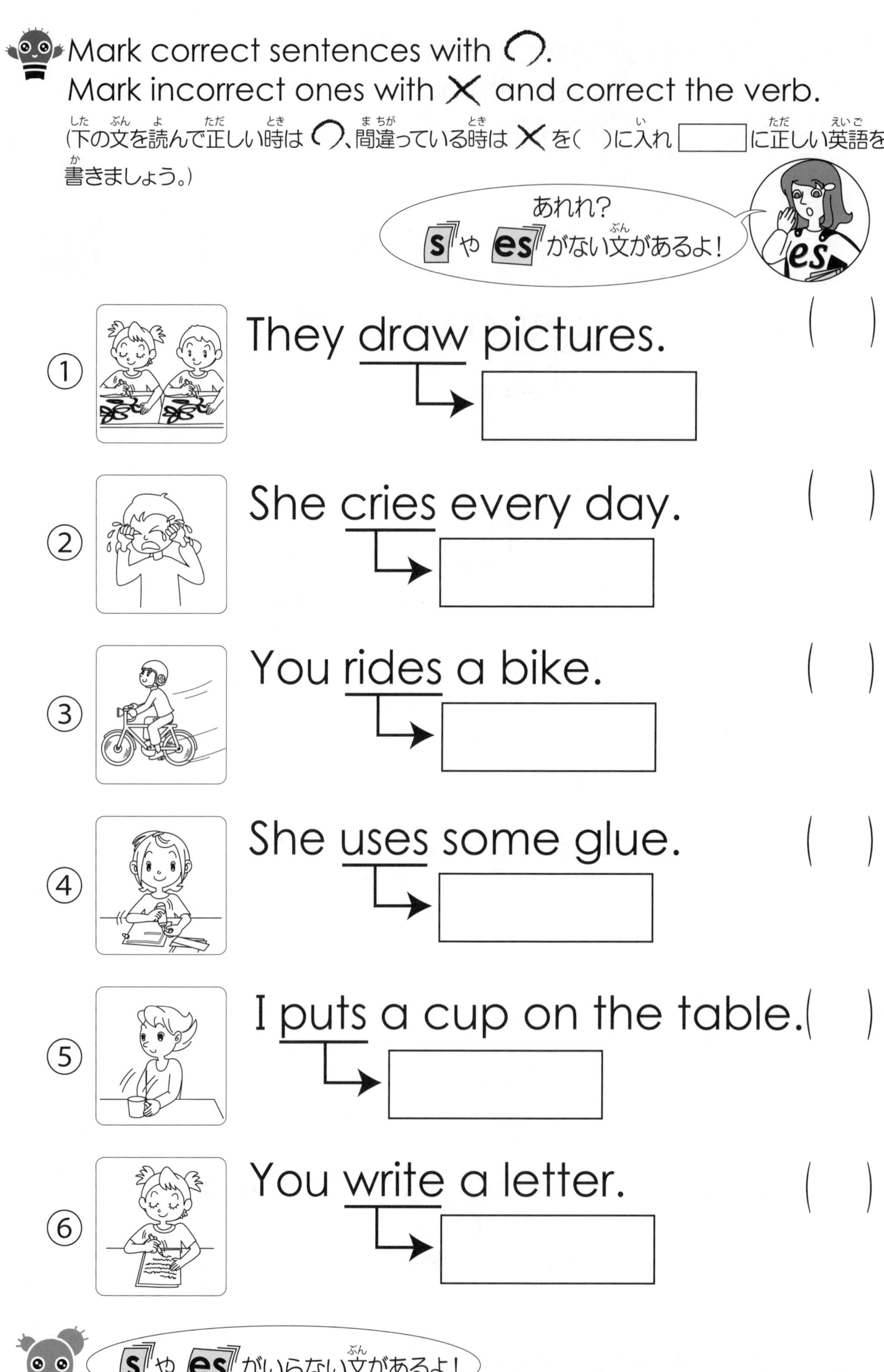

Mark correct sentences with ◯.
Mark incorrect ones with ✕ and correct the verb.
(下の文を読んで正しい時は◯、間違っている時は✕を(　)に入れ□に正しい英語を書きましょう。)

① They draw pictures. (　　)
→ □

② She cries every day. (　　)
→ □

③ You rides a bike. (　　)
→ □

④ She uses some glue. (　　)
→ □

⑤ I puts a cup on the table. (　　)
→ □

⑥ You write a letter. (　　)
→ □

Mark correct sentences with ○.
Mark incorrect ones with ✕ and correct the verb.

(下の文を読んで正しい時は○、間違っている時は✕を(　)に入れ［　　］に正しい英語を書きましょう。)

あれれ？
s や es がない文があるよ！

① He learn to play the piano. → [　　　　] (　　)

② They help me. → [　　　　] (　　)

③ She eat lunch. → [　　　　] (　　)

④ I sleeps at school. → [　　　　] (　　)

⑤ It runs fast. → [　　　　] (　　)

⑥ We pushes the button. → [　　　　] (　　)

s や es がいらない文があるよ！

Section 1 Grammar 1~3 Review 7 Questions & Answers

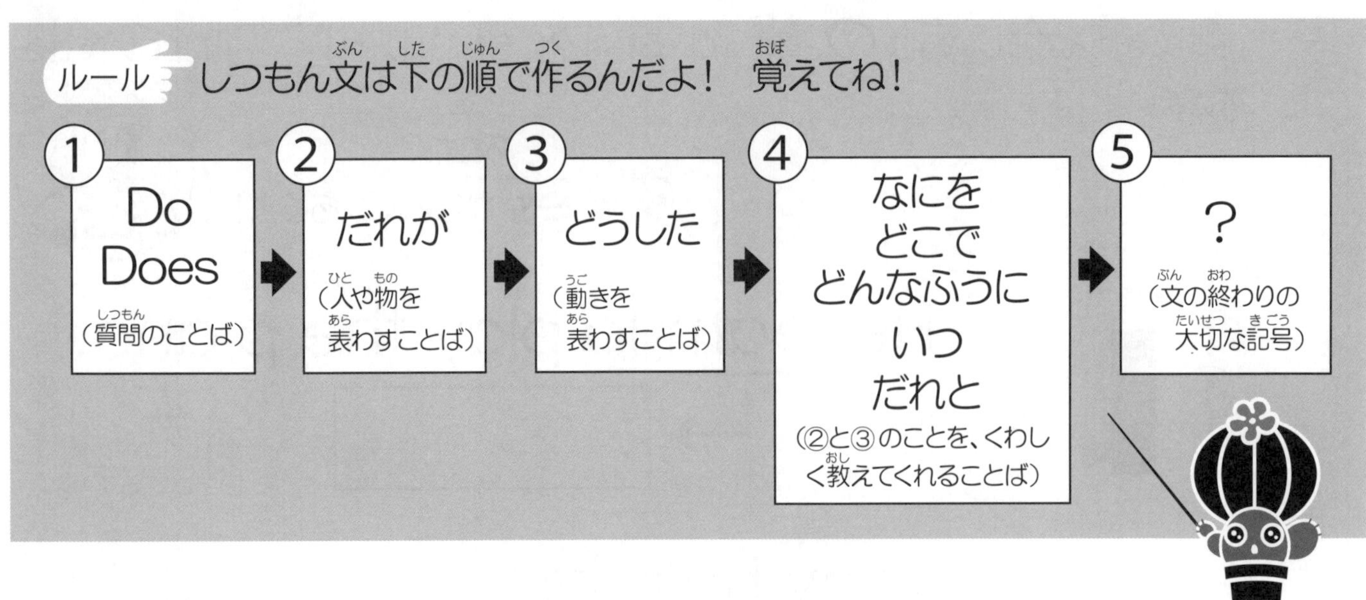

ルール しつもん文は下の順で作るんだよ！ 覚えてね！
1 Do Does (質問のことば)
2 だれが (人や物を表わすことば)
3 どうした (動きを表わすことば)
4 なにを どこで どんなふうに いつ だれと (②と③のことを、くわしく教えてくれることば)
5 ? (文の終わりの大切な記号)

Say it! Let's read the sentences.
(文を読んでみよう！)

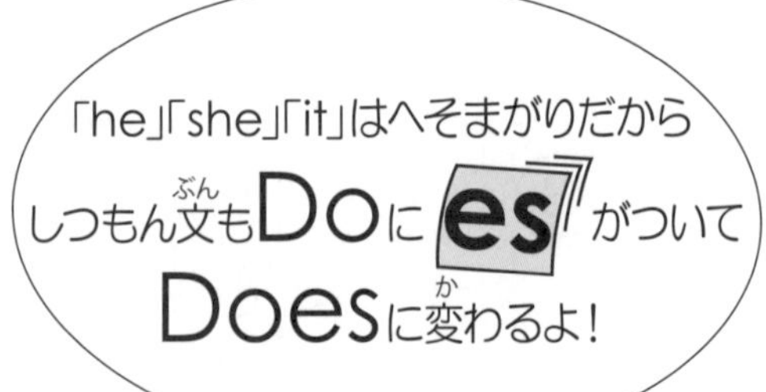

「he」「she」「it」はへそまがりだから
しつもん文もDoにesがついて
Doesに変わるよ！

Do I like cucumbers?

Do you like pears?

Does he like apples?

Does she like watermelons?

Does it like onions?

Do we like melons?

Do you like green peppers?

Do they like oranges?

es
es

Rearrange the words to make a sentence.
((　)の言葉を並べかえて＿＿に正しい文を作ろう!)

【例】

(push / she / ? / the button / Does)

Does she push the button ?

(質問のことば)　(だれが)　(どうした)　(なにを)　(質問の記号)

① (the ball / Do / throw / I / ?)

(質問のことば)　(だれが)　(どうした)　(なにを)　(質問の記号)

② (Does / he / ? / study / math)

(質問のことば)　(だれが)　(どうした)　(なにを)　(質問の記号)

③ (play / ? / soccer / they / Do)

(質問のことば)　(だれが)　(どうした)　(なにを)　(質問の記号)

④ (Does / flowers / ? / she / pick)

(質問のことば)　(だれが)　(どうした)　(なにを)　(質問の記号)

Rearrange the words to make a sentence.
(( )の言葉を並べかえて＿＿に正しい文を作ろう!)

① (she / grapes / eat / ? / Does)

② (Do / ? / use / scissors / we)

③ (brothers / have / Do / they / ?)

④ (? / he / Does / the picture / look / at)

⑤ (at school / teach / Do / you / ?)

⑥ (the piano / Do / learn / I / ?)

Rearrange the words to make a sentence.

((　)の言葉を並べかえて＿＿＿に正しい文を作ろう!)

① (they / Do / ? / drink / milk)

② (Does / she / her mother / ? / help)

③ (wash / the / you / car / ? / Do)

④ (he / a book / read / ? / Does)

⑤ (jump / it / Does / high / ?)

⑥ (ride / ? / we / Do / bikes)

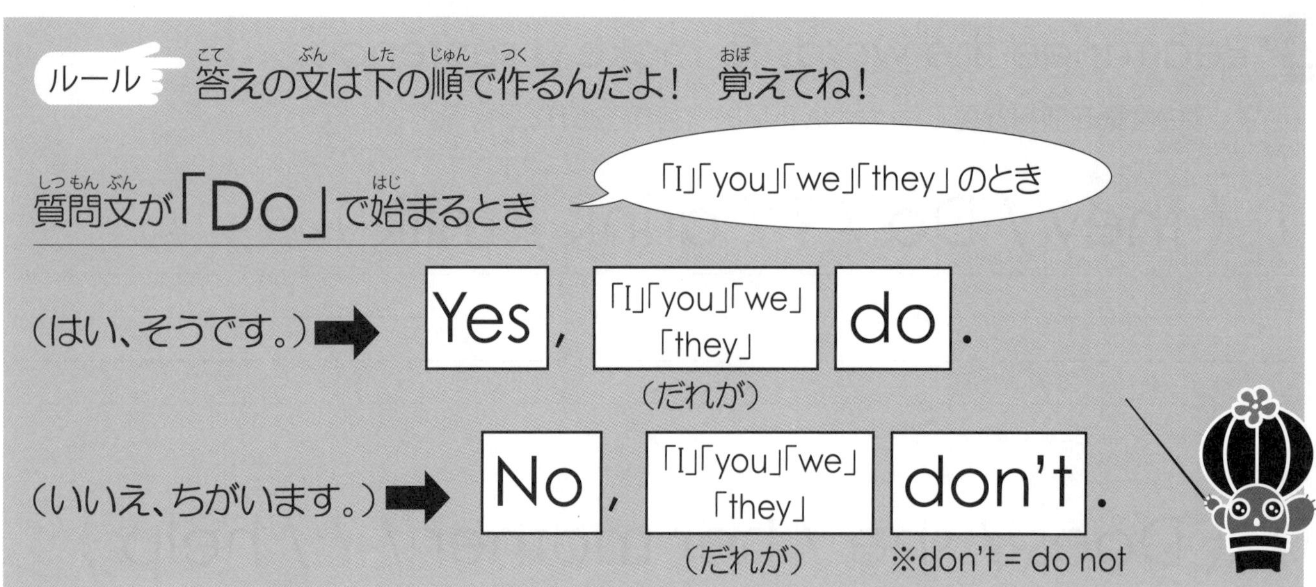

【例】　Do you like apples?

（あなたはりんごがすきですか？）

（はい、すきです）➡ Yes, I do.

（いいえ、すきではありません）➡ No, I don't.

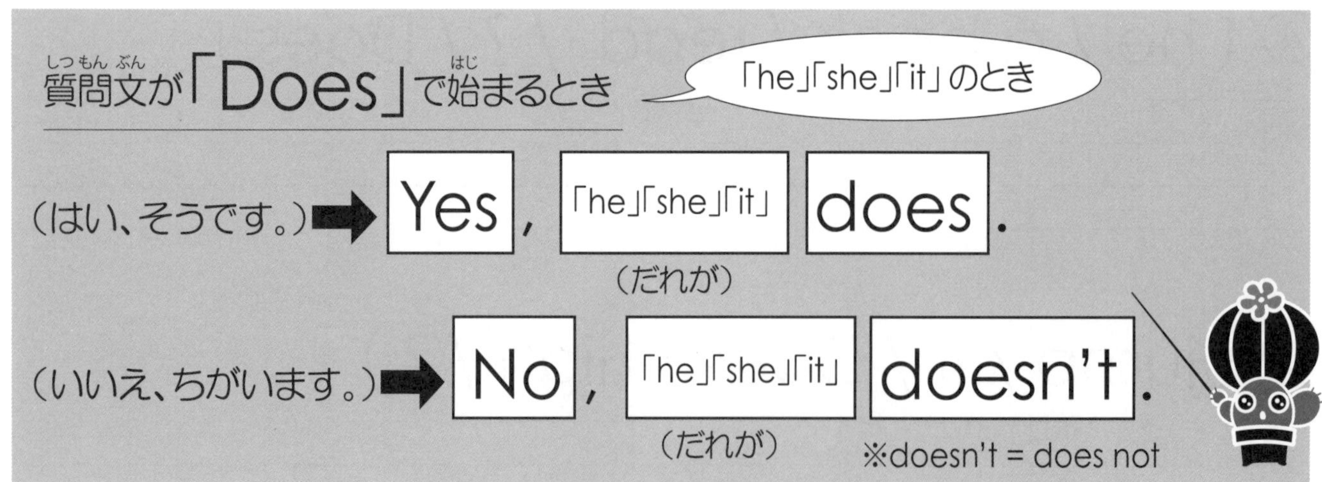

【例】　Does she like apples?

（かのじょはりんごがすきですか？）

（はい、すきです）➡ Yes, she does.

（いいえ、すきではありません）➡ No, she doesn't.

Circle your answers.
(きみはどっち？ あてはまる方に◯をつけよう。)

(質問文)
① Do you like dogs?

(答えの文) Yes, I do. / No, I don't.

② Do you like bananas?

Yes, I do. / No, I don't.

③ Do you like monkeys?

Yes, I do. / No, I don't.

④ Do you like cherries?

Yes, I do. / No, I don't.

⑤ Do you like rabbits?

Yes, I do. / No, I don't.

⑥ Do you like melons?

Yes, I do. / No, I don't.

⑦ Do you like lions?

Yes, I do. / No, I don't.

⑧ Do you like oranges?

Yes, I do. / No, I don't.

Write the missing words on the lines.
（＿＿＿に英語を書いて文を完成させよう！）

「Do」「Does」どちらが入るかな？
線に気を付けて書いてみよう！

(例) ① Does she like dogs?
No, she doesn't.

② ＿＿＿＿ we like coffee?
Yes, we do.

③ ＿＿＿＿ I like watermelons?
Yes, you do.

④ ＿＿＿＿ it like carrots?
Yes, it does.

⑤ ＿＿＿＿ you like rice?
No, I don't.

⑥ ＿＿＿＿ you like cherries?
Yes, I do.

⑦ ＿＿＿＿ he like onions?
No, he doesn't.

⑧ ＿＿＿＿ they like milk?
Yes, they do.

Write the missing words on the lines.
（＿＿に英語を書いて文を完成させよう！）

「Do」「Does」どちらが入るかな？
線に気を付けて書いてみよう！

① ＿＿＿＿＿ it eat cheese?
＿＿＿＿＿, it does.

② ＿＿＿＿＿ you have brothers?
＿＿＿＿＿, we don't.

③ ＿＿＿＿＿ you play soccer?
＿＿＿＿＿, I don't.

④ ＿＿＿＿＿ he live in Japan?
＿＿＿＿＿, he does.

⑤ ＿＿＿＿＿ she like rice?
＿＿＿＿＿, she doesn't.

⑥ ＿＿＿＿＿ they like cherries?
＿＿＿＿＿, they do.

⑦ ＿＿＿＿＿ it like onions?
＿＿＿＿＿, it does.

Section 2 New Basic Verbs

新しい動詞の紹介

Grammar 4
からの新しい動詞だよ!
覚えてね!

Let's read the sentences. (文を読んでみよう!)

① I see the mountain.

② I talk about the movie.

③ I show a map to you.

④ I find an eraser.

⑤ I lose an eraser.

⑥ I finish the class.

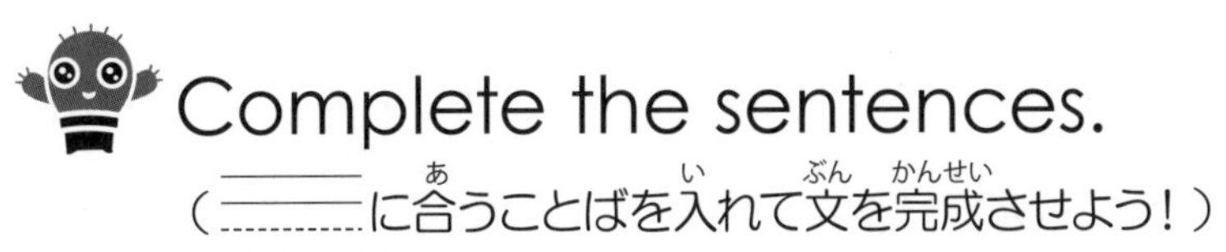

Complete the sentences.

（______に合うことばを入れて文を完成させよう！）

①  I ______ an eraser.

②  I ______ a map to you.

③  I ______ an eraser.

④  I ______ the mountain.

⑤  I ______ the class.

⑥  I ______ about the movie.

Let's read the sentences.（文を読んでみよう！）

Grammar 4
からの新しい動詞だよ！
覚えてね！

① I feel happy.

② I know that boy.

Hello!

③ I say, "Hello."

④ I take you to the park.

⑤ I think about lunch.

⑥ I meet my friend.

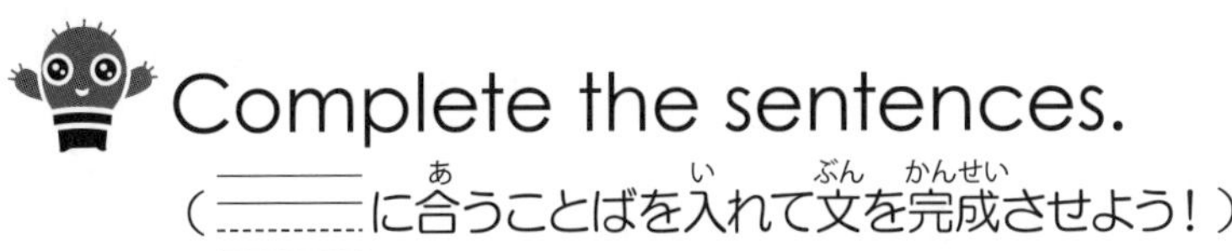

Complete the sentences.

（＿＿＿に合うことばを入れて文を完成させよう！）

①  I ＿＿＿＿＿＿ about lunch.

②  I ＿＿＿＿＿＿ my friend.

③  I ＿＿＿＿＿＿ that boy.

④  I ＿＿＿＿＿＿ you to the park.

⑤ 

I ＿＿＿＿＿＿, “Hello.”

⑥  I ＿＿＿＿＿＿ happy.

Grammar 4
からの新しい動詞だよ！
覚えてね！

Let's read the sentences. (文を読んでみよう！)

① I begin the class.

② I wait for my turn.

③ I clean my room.

4年3組

④ I bring my umbrella to the classroom.

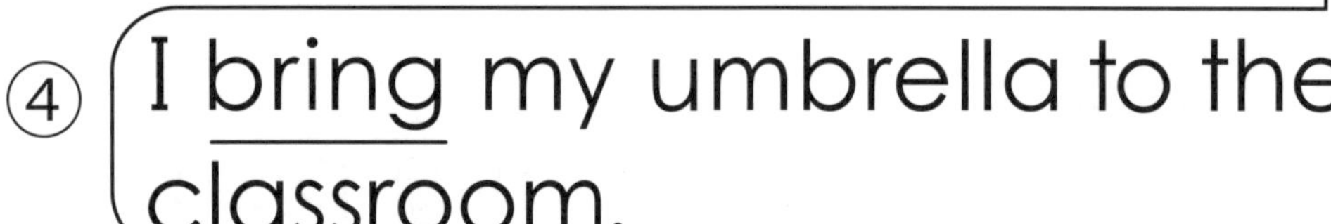

⑤ I tell a story.

⑥ I forget my recorder.

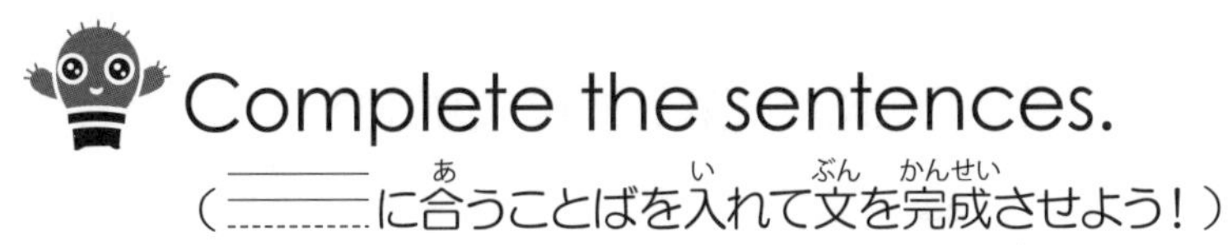

Complete the sentences.

（________に合うことばを入れて文を完成させよう！）

①  I ____________ my umbrella to the classroom.

②  I ____________ my room.

③  I ____________ for my turn.

④  I ____________ my recorder.

⑤  I ____________ the class.

⑥  I ____________ a story.

Match the English words to the Japanese ones.

（英語にあった日本語を選んで線で結ぼう！）

English	Japanese
wait •	• きれいにする
finish •	• 見つける
begin •	• 連れていく
find •	• 会う
take •	• 待つ
meet •	• 終わる
forget •	• 始める
know •	• 知っている
clean •	• 忘れる

Match the English words to the Japanese ones.

（英語(えいご)にあった日本語(にほんご)を選(えら)んで線(せん)で結(むす)ぼう！）

English	Japanese
tell ●	● 見(み)せる
show ●	● 伝(つた)える／言(い)う
lose ●	● 言(い)う
see ●	● なくす
say ●	● 持(も)ってくる
bring ●	● 考(かんが)える
talk ●	● 話(はな)す
feel ●	● 見(み)る
think ●	● 感(かん)じる

Choose the correct word and write it on the lines.

（ ＿＿＿ に英語を書いて文を完成させよう！）

① He ＿＿＿＿＿＿ an eraser.

(find / finds)

② She ＿＿＿＿＿＿ that boy.

(know / knows)

③ He ＿＿＿＿＿＿ the mountain.

(see / sees)

④ They ＿＿＿＿＿＿ their friends.

(meet / meets)

⑤ We ＿＿＿＿＿＿ about the movie.

(talk / talks)

⑥ He ＿＿＿＿＿＿ a map.

(show / shows)

Choose the correct word and write it on the lines.

（ ＿＿＿ に英語を書いて文を完成させよう！）

① A teacher ______________ the class.

(begin / begins)

② I __________ happy.

(feel / feels)

③ Students ______________ for their turn.

(wait / waits)

④ A boy ______________ his flute.

(forget / forgets)

⑤ A girl ______________ her umbrella.

(bring / brings)

⑥ I __________ you to the park.

(take / takes)

Choose the correct word and write it on the lines.

（ ＿＿＿ に英語(えいご)を書(か)いて文(ぶん)を完成(かんせい)させよう！）

① My brother ______________ me a map.

(show / shows)

② I __________ , “Hello.”

(say / says)

③ We ______________ the class.

(finish / finishes)

④ I __________ about lunch.

(think / thinks)

⑤ A boy ______________ an eraser.

(lose / loses)

⑥ My mother ______________ a story.

(tell / tells)

Complete the questions by adding the correct question word and choosing a verb.

(正しい言葉を下から選んで ______ の上に書き、文を完成させよう。ただし、質問の時に使われる一語が不足しているので加えてね。)

① 彼女はさよならを言いますか？

______ she ______ "Goodbye"?

② 私たちは駅で会いますか？

______ we ______ at the station ?

③ 私は彼女を待ちますか？

______ I ______ for her ?

④ 彼らはその箱を持っていますか？

______ they ______ the boxes ?

⑤ 彼はカバンを忘れますか？

______ he ______ a bag ?

⑥ あなたは彼女を公園に連れて行きますか？

______ you ______ her to the park ?

⑦ あなたは彼を知っていますか？

______ you ______ him ?

say / forget / know / have

meet / take / wait

今
Now

未来
Future

上の▨で行なわれたことは過去(終わったこと)のことだね。
それを表わす英語をここでは練習しよう！

過去(終わったこと)を表わす時は

『ごはんを きのう 食べる。』とは言わないね。➡ 『食べた。』になるよね。

英語も終わったことを表わす時は言葉が少し変わるんだよ！

≪時を表わすことば≫

ルール 次のことばが文中にあったら『過去(終わったこと)』を表わしているんだよ。

yesterday	(きのう)
last night	(きのうの夜)
last Monday	(先週の月曜日)
last week	(先週)
last month	(先月)
last year	(さく年／きょ年)
～ ago	(～前)

Choose the correct picture from Ⓐ to Ⓒ.

(次の文の表わす絵は下のどれかな？ Ⓐ～Ⓒから選んで○をつけよう！)

Ⓐ Past 過去 — Now 今 — Future 未来

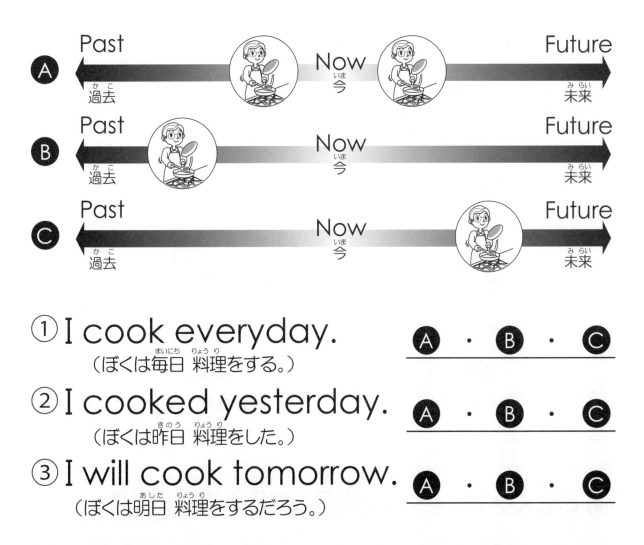

Ⓑ Past 過去 — Now 今 — Future 未来

Ⓒ Past 過去 — Now 今 — Future 未来

① I cook everyday. Ⓐ・Ⓑ・Ⓒ

（ぼくは毎日 料理をする。）

② I cooked yesterday. Ⓐ・Ⓑ・Ⓒ

（ぼくは昨日 料理をした。）

③ I will cook tomorrow. Ⓐ・Ⓑ・Ⓒ

（ぼくは明日 料理をするだろう。）

過去を表わす動詞のことを学ぼう。

I cook everyday. ➡ I cooked yesterday.

（ぼくは毎日 料理を する 。） ➡ （ぼくは昨日 料理を した 。）

上の文でわかるように終わった事を表わす時には、動詞の形がかわるよ！

「**cook**」が「**cooked**」に変身すると

「**～する**」が「**～した**」ということばになるよ！

過去を表わす動詞のことを学ぼう！

ルール

I cook*ed* yesterday.

ぼくは昨日 料理を**した**。（「料理を**する**」ではないよ！）

≪動詞を過去のことばに変身することを助ける2人≫

ed
d
ied
?
忍
きそく
ふきそく
「きそくクン」
「ふきそくチャン」

【例】**きそくクン**の場合… **次の3つの形に変身!!**

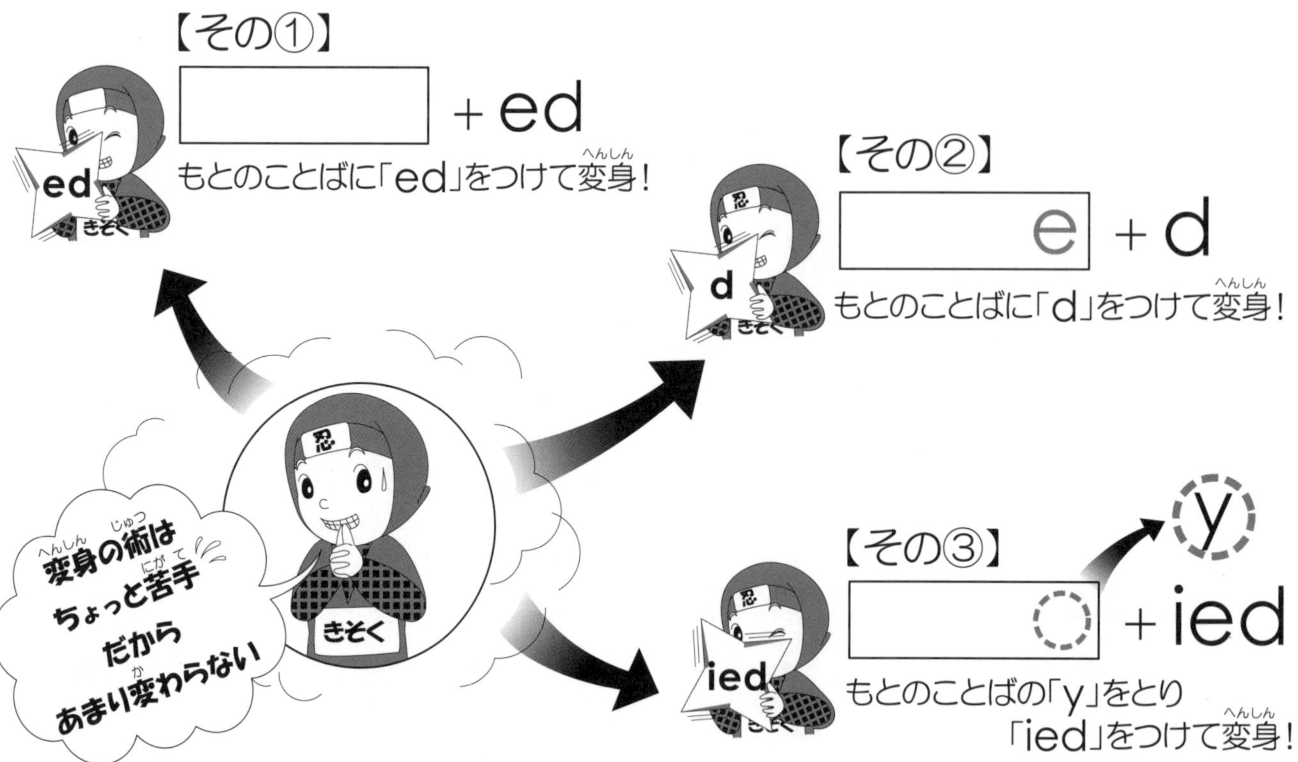

【その①】
＋ed
もとのことばに「ed」をつけて変身！
【その②】
e ＋d
もとのことばに「d」をつけて変身！
【その③】
y
＋ied
もとのことばの「y」をとり
「ied」をつけて変身！
変身の術は
ちょっと苦手
だから
あまり変わらない
ed
d
ied
きそく

きそくクンが登場することばを練習してみよう!

きそく

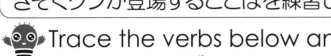

Trace the verbs below and write the Japanese in the ( ). (次の ____ のことばをなぞって( )に日本語をかこう!)

【その①】

[ ] + ed

もとの形に『ed』をつけるだけでOKだよ!

cook (料理する) → cooked ( )

watch (見る) → watched ( )

help (手伝う) → helped ( )

open (開ける) → opened ( )

【その②】

[e] + d

これはとくべつ!
もともと最後に『e』がついている時は『d』をつけるだけでOKだよ!

close (閉める) → closed ( )

move (動く) → moved ( )

live (住む) → lived ( )

【その③】

[y] + ied

これはとくべつ!
最後の『y』を『i』に変えてから『ed』をつけるんだよ!

study (勉強する) → studied ( )

【例】ふきそくチャンの場合…

覚えたかな？
次のページからは
自分で書くよ！
なんども
練習してみよう！！

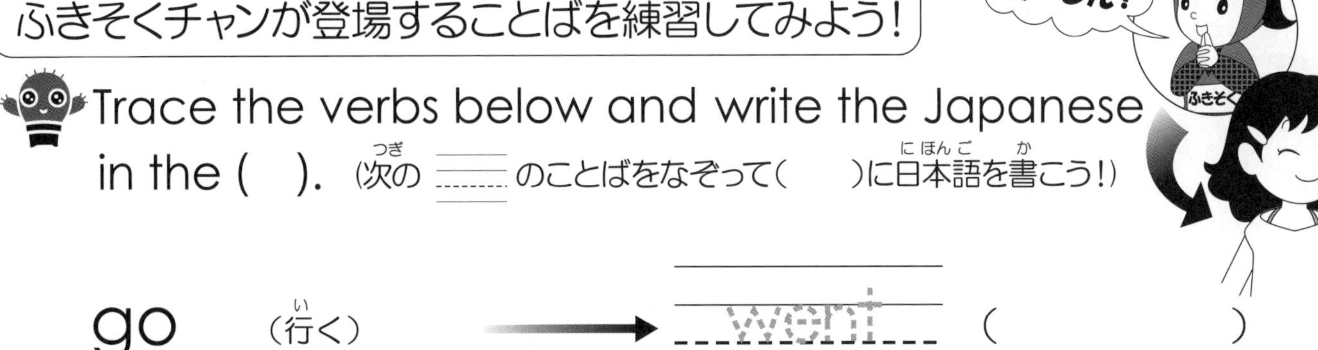

ふきそくチャンが登場することばを練習してみよう！

Trace the verbs below and write the Japanese in the (　). (次の ＿＿ のことばをなぞって(　　)に日本語を書こう！)

go	(行く)	→	went	(　　　　)
run	(走る)	→	ran	(　　　　)
have	(持つ)	→	had	(　　　　)
drink	(飲む)	→	drank	(　　　　)
eat	(食べる)	→	ate	(　　　　)
see	(見る)	→	saw	(　　　　)
sit	(座る)	→	sat	(　　　　)
come	(来る)	→	came	(　　　　)
get	(手に入れる)	→	got	(　　　　)
write	(書く)	→	wrote	(　　　　)

ルール 「He•She•Itはへそまがり」って Grammar 3 で学んだよね。
だから、下のようになるのは覚えているかな？

He ~~walk~~ ⟶ He walks

She ~~walk~~ ⟶ She walks

It ~~walk~~ ⟶ It walks

でも過去形（終わった事を表わす）では「he」「she」「it」でも
動詞は全て同じように変身するんだよ！

【例】きそくクンの場合…

I walk ⟶ I walk**ed**

You walk ⟶ You walk**ed**

He walk**s** ⟶ He walk**ed**

She walk**s** ⟶ She walk**ed**

It walk**s** ⟶ It walk**ed**

We walk ⟶ We walk**ed**

They walk ⟶ They walk**ed**

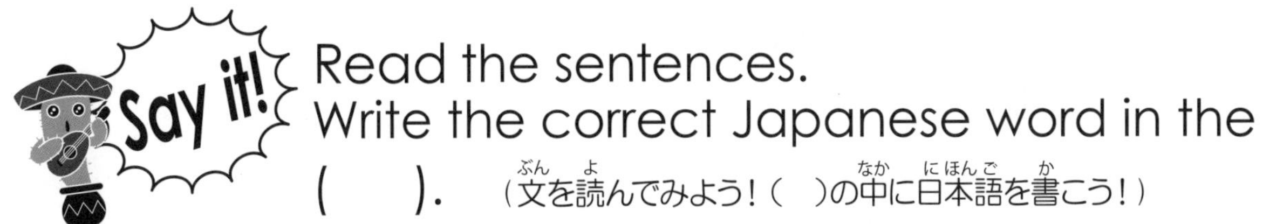

Read the sentences.
Write the correct Japanese word in the ( ). （文を読んでみよう！（　）の中に日本語を書こう！）

① I help**ed** my mother yesterday.
(　　　　)

② You watch**ed** TV yesterday.
(　　　　)

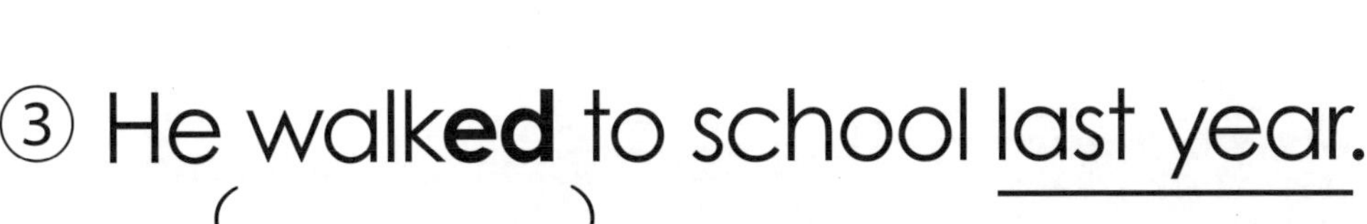
③ He walk**ed** to school last year.
(　　　　)

④ She cook**ed** dinner last month.
(　　　　)

⑤ It open**ed** the door last night.
(　　　　)

⑥ We liv**ed** in Japan two years ago.
(　　　　)

⑦ You stud**ied** English last Monday.
(　　　　)

⑧ They us**ed** the ball last week.
(　　　　)

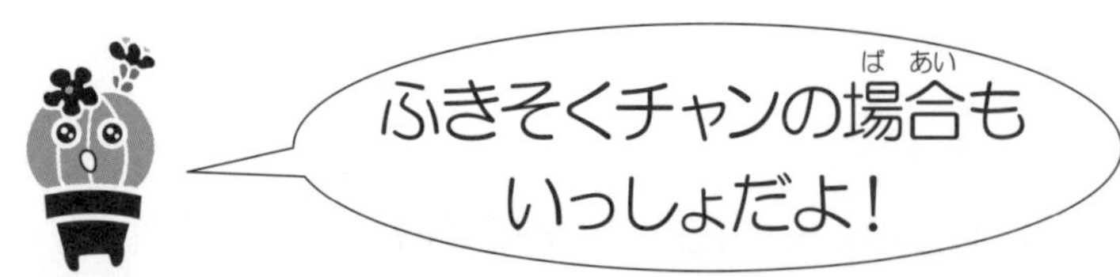

ルール 「He•She•Itはへそまがり」って Grammar 3 で学んだよね。だから、下のようになるのは覚えているかな？

He ~~go~~ ⟶ He goes

She ~~go~~ ⟶ She goes

It ~~go~~ ⟶ It goes

でも過去形（終わった事を表わす）では「he」「she」「it」でも動詞は全て同じように変身するんだよ！

【例】ふきそくチャンの場合…

変～しん！

I go ⟶ I went

You go ⟶ You went

He go**es** ⟶ He went

She go**es** ⟶ She went

It go**es** ⟶ It went

We go ⟶ We went

They go ⟶ They went

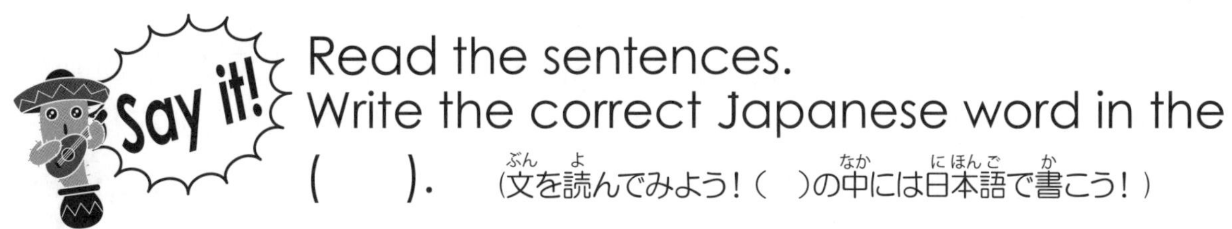

Read the sentences.
Write the correct Japanese word in the ( ). (文を読んでみよう！（　）の中には日本語で書こう！）

① I **went** to school yesterday.
(　　　　　)

② You **ran** in the park last week.
(　　　　　)

③ He **had** a balloon yesterday.
(　　　　　)

④ She **drank** some milk last night.
(　　　　　)

⑤ It **ate** some food 30 minutes ago.
(　　　　　)

⑥ We **saw** the castle last year.
(　　　　　)

⑦ You **sat** on the sofa yesterday.
(　　　　　)

⑧ They **came** from China last week.
(　　　　　)

Trace the verbs below and read the sentences.
（正しい形でなぞって書いたら、読んでみよう！）

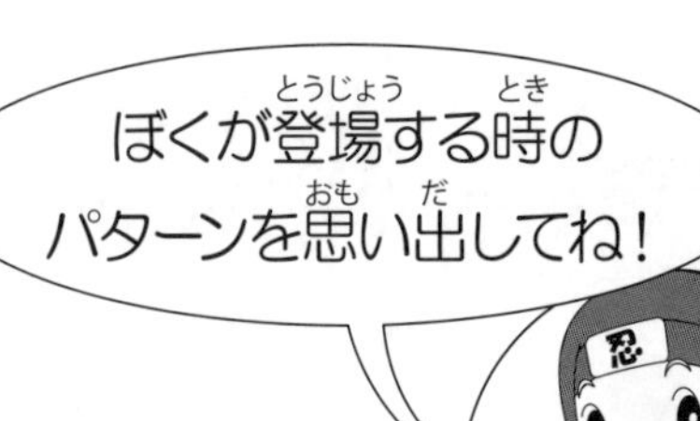
ぼくが登場する時の
パターンを思い出してね！
きそく

① They talk about TV every day.

↘

They talked about TV last night.

とくべつだったね！
『d』をつけるだけでOKだよ！
d

② I live in Japan.

↘

I lived in Japan last year.

へそまがりの『s』は外して
『ed』をつけるんだよ！

③ She wants a new dress every day.

↘

She wanted a new dress last week.

④ You learn a new song every day.

↘

You learned a new song last Monday.

Trace the verbs below and read the sentences.
（正しい形でなぞって書いたら、読んでみよう！）

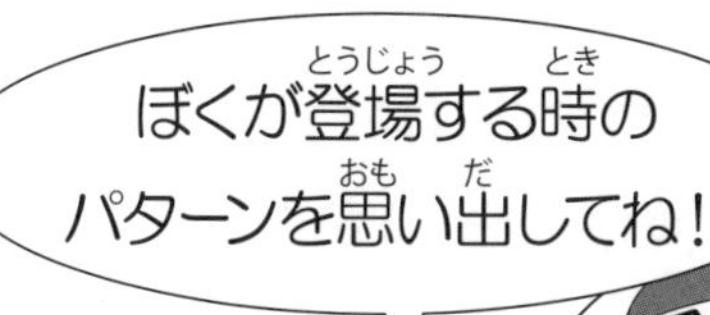
ぼくが登場する時の
パターンを思い出してね！

忍
きそく

①I close the curtains every day.

I closed the curtains last night.

②We wash the dishes every day.

We washed the dishes yesterday.

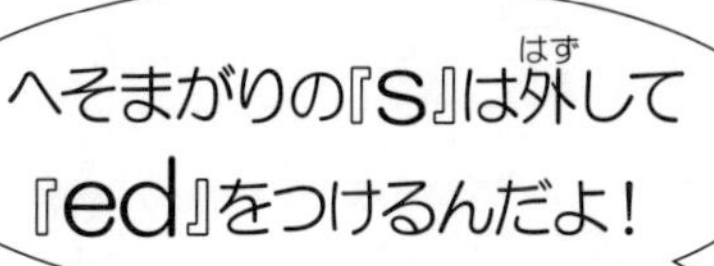
へそまがりの『s』は外して
『ed』をつけるんだよ！

③He plays soccer every day.

He played soccer two days ago.

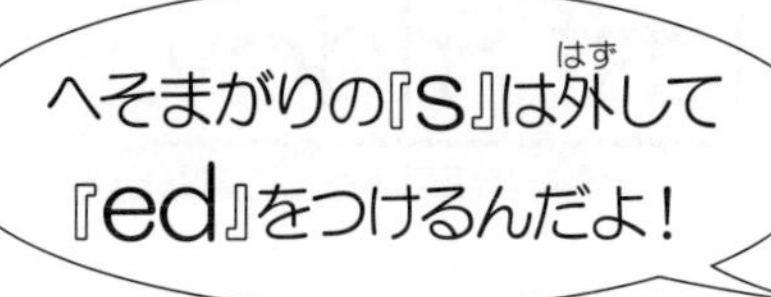
へそまがりの『s』は外して
『ed』をつけるんだよ！

④She walks to school every day.

She walked to school yesterday.

Trace the verbs below and read the sentences.
(正しい形でなぞって書いたら、読んでみよう！)

ぼくが登場する時の
パターンを思い出してね！
きそく

①She opens the box every day.

She opened the box last year.

へそまがりの『s』は外して
『ed』をつけるんだよ！

②I watch TV every day.

I watched TV yesterday.

へそまがりの『s』は外して
『ed』をつけるんだよ！

③He shows the map to you every day.

He showed the map to you last Friday.

④You pull the dog every day.

You pulled the dog last night.

Trace the verbs below and read the sentences.
（正しい形でなぞって書いたら、読んでみよう！）

ぼくが登場する時のパターンを思い出してね！

とくべつだったね！
『d』をつけるだけでOKだよ！

① She uses glue every day.

She used glue last week.

最後の『y』を『i』に変えてから『ed』をつけるんだよ！

とくべつだよね！

② I study English every day.

I studied English last year.

へそまがりの『s』は外すよ！

とくべつだったね！
『d』をつけるだけでOKだよ！

③ He moves the chair every day.

He moved the chair last month.

へそまがりの『s』は外して
『ed』をつけるんだよ！

④ She cooks dinner every day.

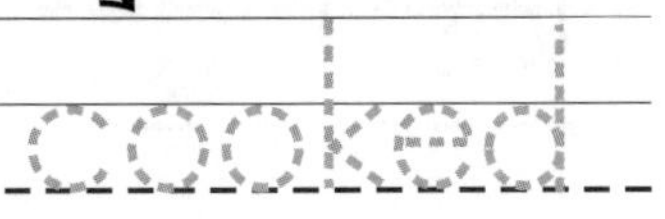

She cooked dinner last night.

Trace the verbs below and read the sentences.
（正しい形でなぞって書いたら、読んでみよう！）

わたしは
変身がとくい！
全然ちがう形に
変わるよ。
ふきそく

①She runs in the park every day.

She ran in the park last year.

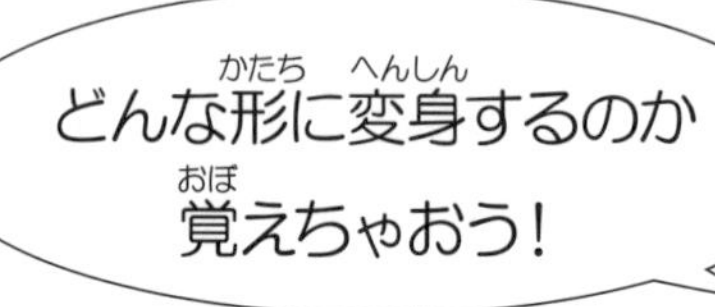
どんな形に変身するのか
覚えちゃおう！

②I have a class every day.

I had a class yesterday.

③He eats curry and rice every day.

He ate curry and rice last Friday.

④You see the dog every day.

You saw the dog last night.

Trace the verbs below and read the sentences.
(正しい形でなぞって書いたら、読んでみよう！)

わたしは
変身がとくい！
全然ちがう形に
変わるよ。
忍
ふきそく

①I go to school every day.

I went to school last year.

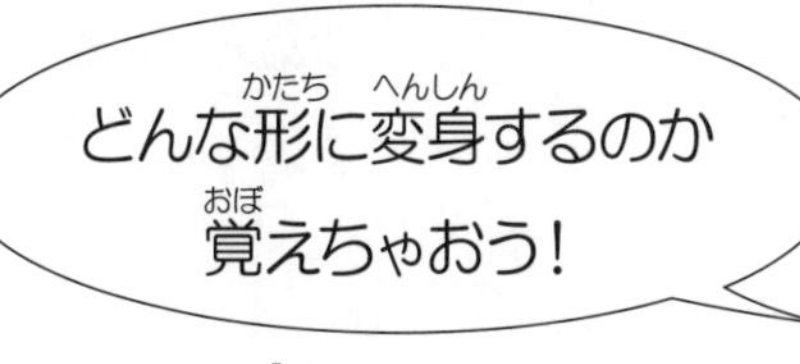
どんな形に変身するのか
覚えちゃおう！

②She drinks some milk every day.

She drank some milk 30 minutes ago.

③He sits in the front seat every day.

He sat in the front seat last Friday.

④You write a letter every day.

You wrote a letter last night.

Section 4 How to Make Past Tense Questions & Answers

過去形の質問文と答えの文

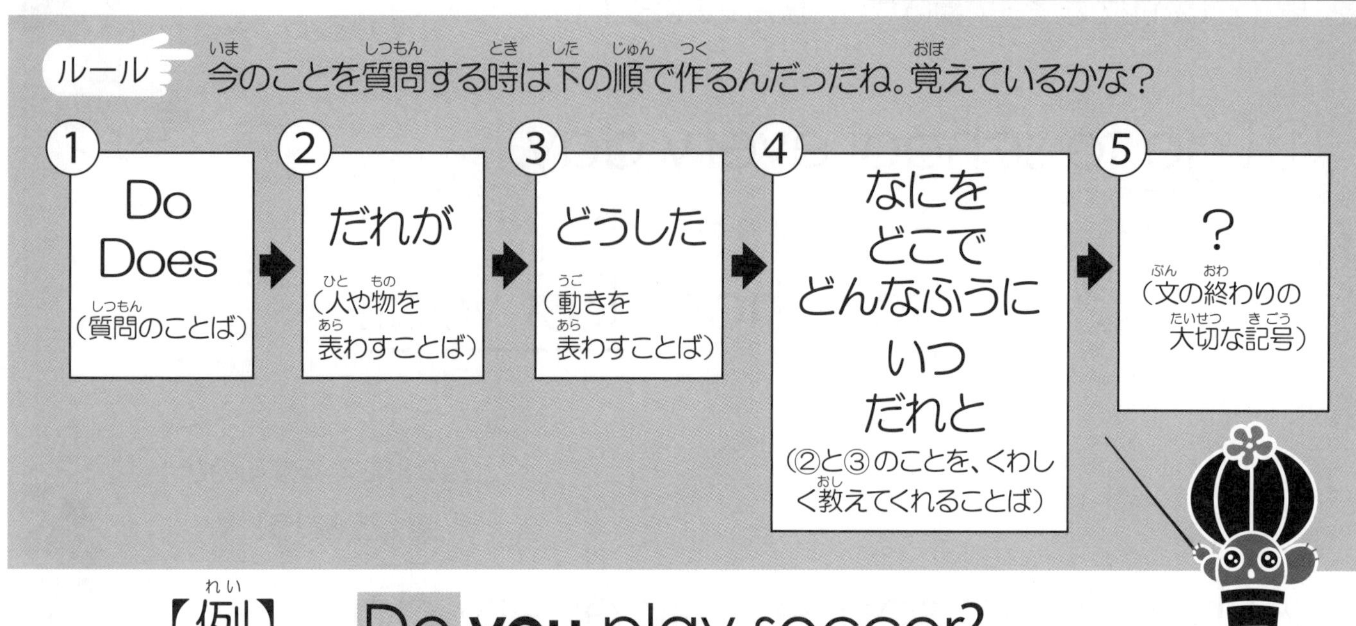

ルール
今のことを質問する時は下の順で作るんだったね。覚えているかな？
① Do Does（質問のことば）
② だれが（人や物を表わすことば）
③ どうした（動きを表わすことば）
④ なにを どこで どんなふうに いつ だれと（②と③のことを、くわしく教えてくれることば）
⑤ ？（文の終わりの大切な記号）

【例】 Do **you** play soccer?

Does **he** play soccer?

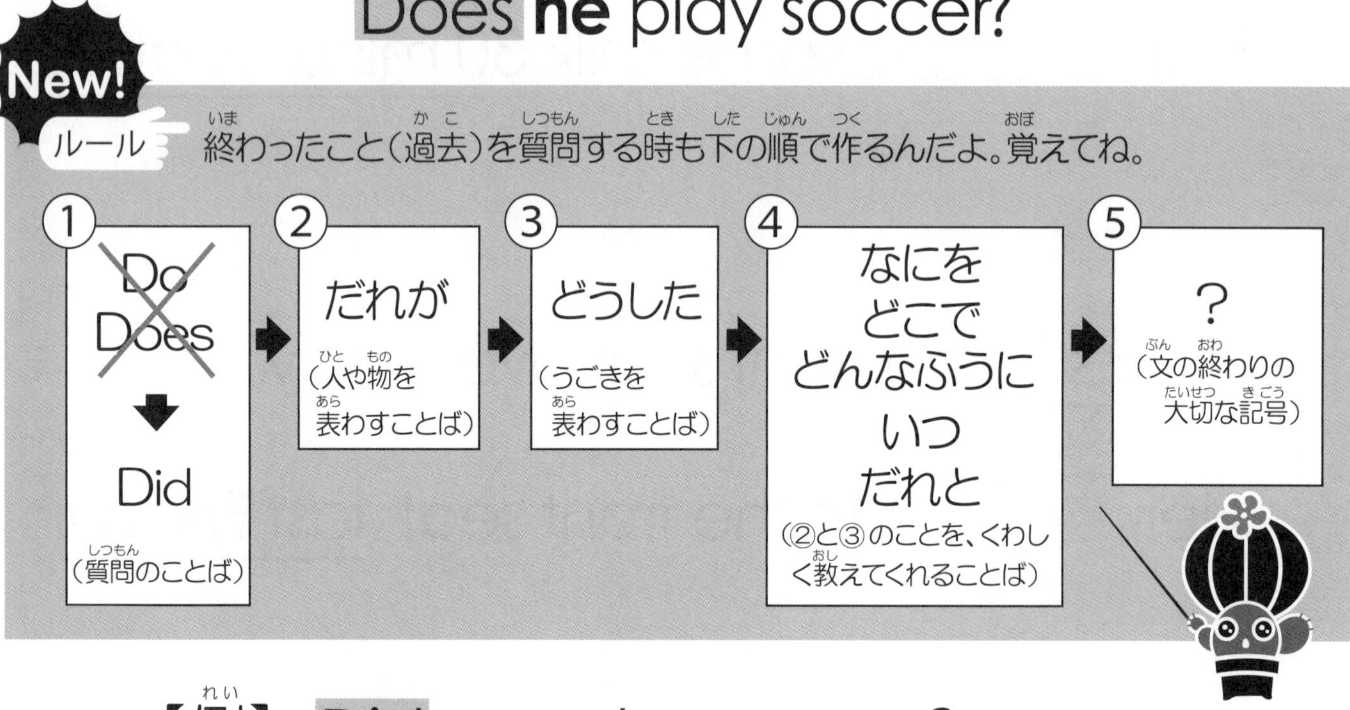

New!
ルール
終わったこと（過去）を質問する時も下の順で作るんだよ。覚えてね。
① Do Does → Did（質問のことば）
② だれが（人や物を表わすことば）
③ どうした（うごきを表わすことば）
④ なにを どこで どんなふうに いつ だれと（②と③のことを、くわしく教えてくれることば）
⑤ ？（文の終わりの大切な記号）

【例】 Did **you** play soccer?

Didサムライ参上！

～しましたか？

Did **he** play soccer?

もとの形のままだよ！

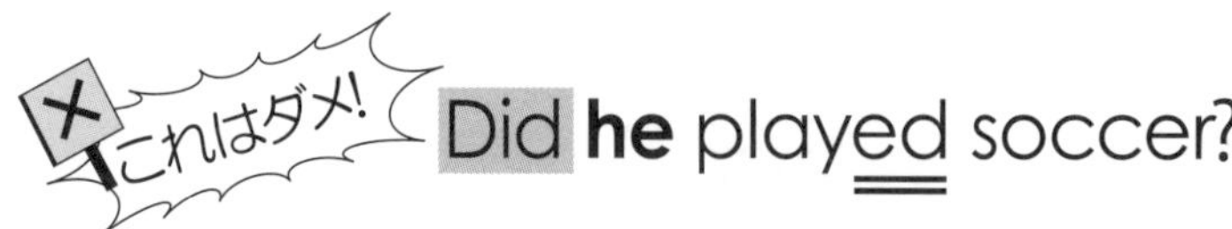

✕ これはダメ!
Did **he** played soccer?

≪質問文≫

Did が登場したら
cleaned ⇒ clean にもどるよ!
he, she, it でも clean~~s~~ だよ!

I cleaned the room.

（わたしは部屋をきれいにしました）

Read the sentences.
（文を読んでみよう！）

Did I clean the room?

Did you clean the room?

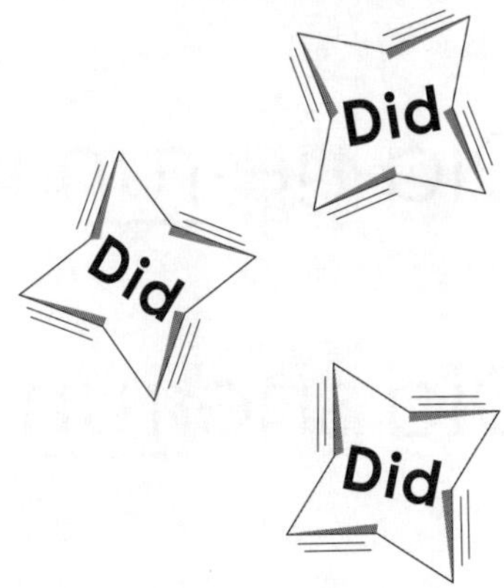

Did he clean the room?

Did she clean the room?

Did it clean the room?

Did we clean the room?

Did you clean the room?

Did they clean the room?

≪質問文≫

Did が登場したら
ran ⇒ run にもどるよ!
he, she, it でも runs̶ だよ!

I ran in the park.

(わたしは公園を走りました)

Read the sentences.
(文を読んでみよう!)

Did I run in the park?

Did you run in the park?

Did he run in the park?

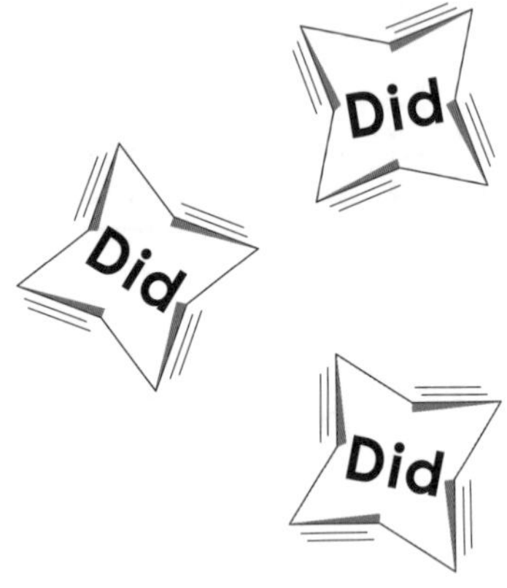

Did she run in the park?

Did it run in the park?

Did we run in the park?

Did you run in the park?

Did they run in the park?

Circle the correct words.

（正しいことばに ◯ をつけよう。）

『～しましたか？』
と質問しているよ！

① Did you (study / studied) English **yesterday**?

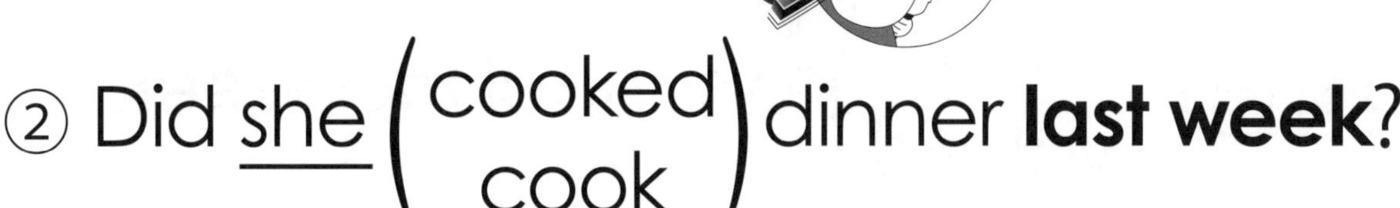
Did
基本の形の動詞を選んでね！！

② Did she (cooked / cook) dinner **last week**?

③ Did he (close / closed) the door **yesterday**?

④ Did you (use / used) some glue **yesterday**?

⑤ Did they (lived / live) in Japan **last year**?

⑥ Did we (wash / washed) the dishes **last night**?

Circle the correct words.

(正しいことばに ◯ をつけよう。)

『～しましたか？』
と質問しているよ！

① Did you (talked / talk) to him **yesterday**?

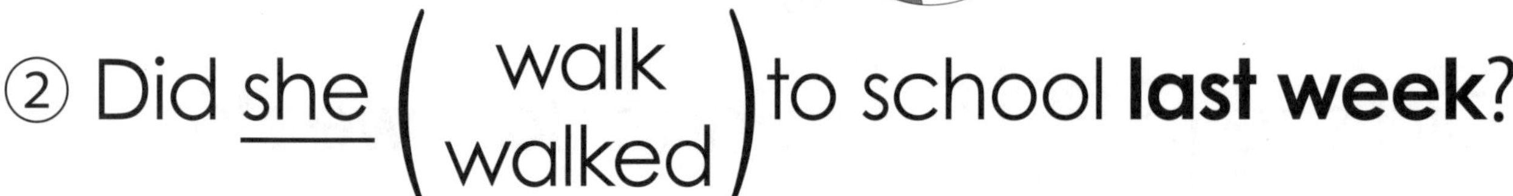
Did
基本の形の動詞を選んでね!!

② Did she (walk / walked) to school **last week**?

③ Did my brother (play / played) soccer **yesterday**?

④ Did they (watched / watch) TV **last Monday**?

⑤ Did you (listened / listen) to a CD **yesterday**?

⑥ Did my sister (help / helped) him **last night**?

① Did you (drink / drank) orange juice **yesterday**?

Did

基本の形の動詞を選んでね！！

② Did he (go / went) to school **yesterday**?

③ Did the cat (ran / run) in the park **yesterday**?

④ Did we (saw / see) the dog **last Monday**?

⑤ Did you (eat / ate) dinner **last night?**

⑥ Did my uncle (wrote / write) a letter **yesterday**?

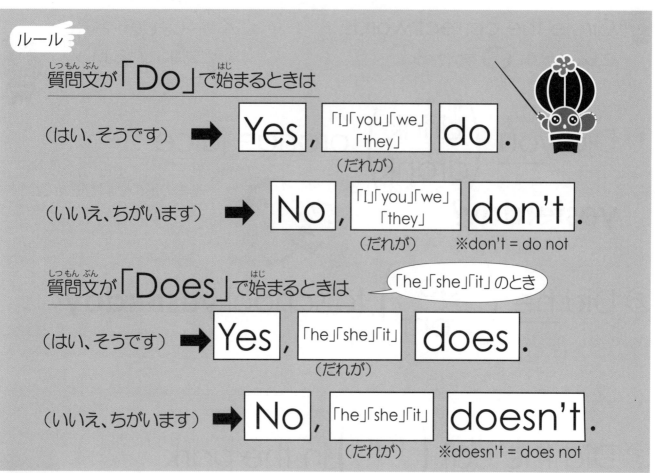

ルール

質問文が「Do」で始まるときは

（はい、そうです） ➡ Yes, 「I」「you」「we」「they」（だれが） do.

（いいえ、ちがいます） ➡ No, 「I」「you」「we」「they」（だれが） don't.

※don't = do not

質問文が「Does」で始まるときは

「he」「she」「it」のとき

（はい、そうです） ➡ Yes, 「he」「she」「it」（だれが） does.

（いいえ、ちがいます） ➡ No, 「he」「she」「it」（だれが） doesn't.

※doesn't = does not

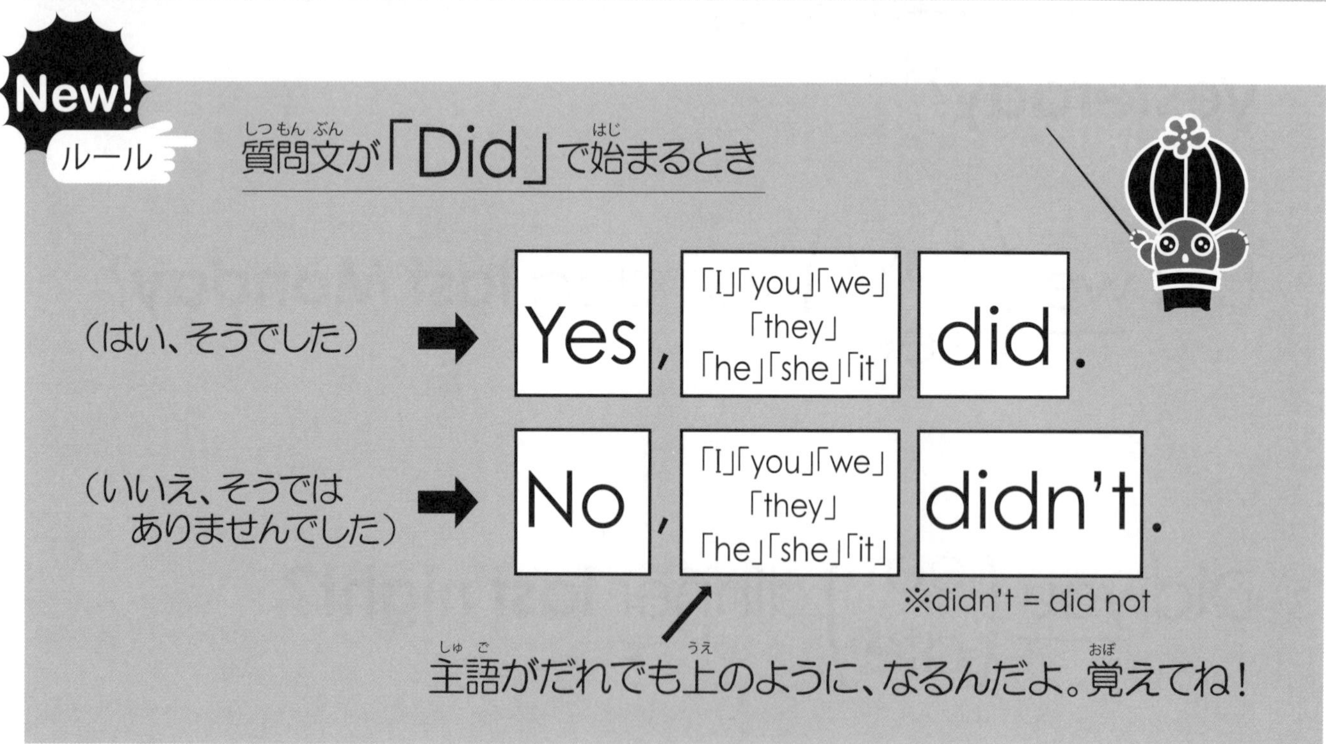
New!

ルール

質問文が「Did」で始まるとき

（はい、そうでした） ➡ Yes, 「I」「you」「we」「they」「he」「she」「it」 did.

（いいえ、そうではありませんでした） ➡ No, 「I」「you」「we」「they」「he」「she」「it」 didn't.

※didn't = did not

主語がだれでも上のように、なるんだよ。覚えてね！

【例】Did you play soccer? （サッカーをしましたか？）

Yes, I **did**.  （はい、しました）

No, I **didn't**.  （いいえ、しませんでした）

Read the sentences.（文を読んでみよう！）

【例】Did you study yesterday?

Yes, I did.

No, I didn't.

(※didn't = did not)

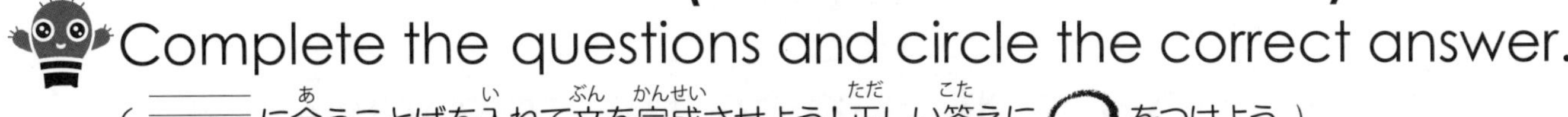

Complete the questions and circle the correct answer.

（＿＿に合うことばを入れて文を完成させよう！正しい答えに〇をつけよう。）

① __________ you cook yesterday?

Yes, I (did / didn't).

② __________ he walk to school yesterday?

Yes, he (did / didn't).

③ __________ she watch TV yesterday?

No, she (did / didn't).

④ __________ they sing a song yesterday?

No, they (did / didn't).

Ask your friends the questions and circle their answers.
(お友達に次の質問をしてみよう! 答えに◯をつけてみよう!)

① Did you study yesterday?

Yes, I did.

No, I didn't.

② Did you eat lunch yesterday?

Yes, I did.

No, I didn't.

③ Did you watch TV yesterday?

Yes, I did.

No, I didn't.

④ Did you ride a bike yesterday?

Yes, I did.

No, I didn't.

⑤ Did you play baseball yesterday?

Yes, I did.

No, I didn't.

⑥ Did you read a book yesterday?

Yes, I did.

No, I didn't.

Complete the questions and circle the correct answer.
（______に合うことばを入れて文を完成させよう！正しい答えに◯をつけよう。）

① __________ you speak to him yesterday?

No, I (did / didn't).

② __________ she use some glue yesterday?

No, she (did / didn't).

③ __________ they swim yesterday?

Yes, they (did / didn't).

④ __________ you listen to a CD yesterday?

No, I (did / didn't).

⑤ __________ she learn a new song yesterday?

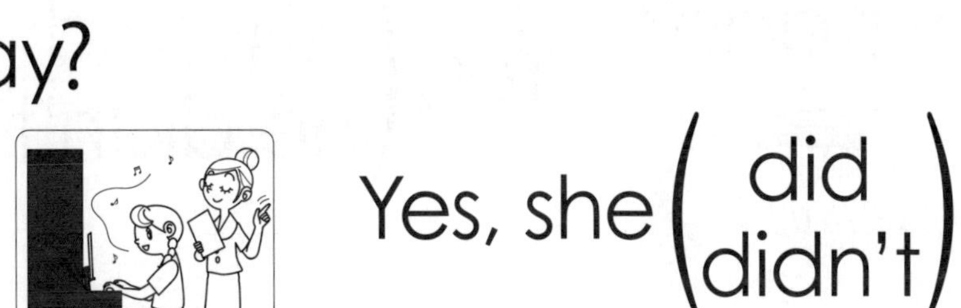
Yes, she (did / didn't).

Circle the correct answer.

（正[ただ]しい答[こた]えに ◯ をつけよう。）

① Did you give a present to me last year?

Yes, (I did / you didn't).

② Did she run to school last week?

No, (he did / she didn't).

③ Did my uncle sing yesterday?

Yes, (he did / we didn't).

④ Did they make a cake last Monday?

No, (we did / they didn't).

⑤ Did my aunt come to Japan two days ago?

Yes, (she did / he didn't).

Complete the sentences.（＿＿に合うことばを入れて文を完成させよう！）

【例】 Did they play soccer yesterday?

Yes, they did.

① ________ you watch TV yesterday?

Yes, ________________

② ________ he find an eraser yesterday?

Yes, ________________

③ ________ she cook yesterday?

Yes, ________________

Complete the sentences. （＿＿に合うことばを入れて文を完成させよう！）

【例】 Did she wash the dishes yesterday?

No, she didn't.

① ＿＿＿ you sell vegetables yesterday?

No, ＿＿＿＿＿＿＿＿

② ＿＿＿ they talk yesterday?

No, ＿＿＿＿＿＿＿＿

③ ＿＿＿ he study math yesterday?

No, ＿＿＿＿＿＿＿＿

Complete the sentences. （　　に合うことばを入れて文を完成させよう！）

①Did you learn a new song yesterday?

Yes,

②Did you forget your book yesterday?

No,

③Did you hear birds yesterday?

No,

④Did you listen to the CD yesterday?

Yes,

⑤Did you close a curtains yesterday?

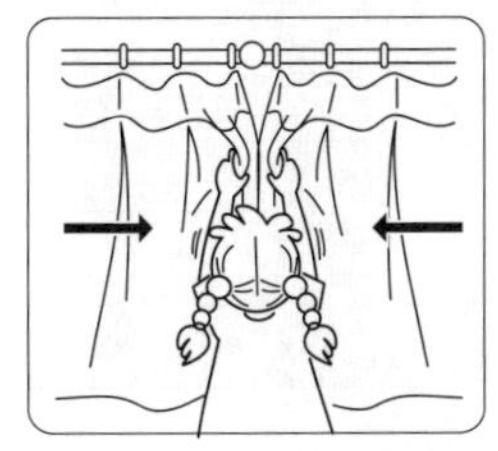

Yes,

Complete the sentences.（ に合うことばを入れて文を完成させよう！）

①Did you sleep well last night?

No,

②Did you pick flowers yesterday?

Yes,

③Did you climb a tree yesterday?

No,

④Did you show a map to me yesterday?

No,

⑤Did you touch the dog yesterday?

Yes,

スペシャル問題!!
Special Challenge!

Read the sentences. Then write your own answers on the lines.

(次の文を読んで、“君はきのう何をした”のかを ＿＿ に英語でかこう!)

※下の ＿＿ の言葉を使ってもいいよ!

What **did** you do yesterday?
きのう君は何したの?
I play**ed** soccer yesterday.
What **did** you do yesterday?
I ______________________.
I ______________________.
I ______________________.

watched TV	played with friends
studied math	washed the dishes

Section 5 | Grammar 2, 3 Review 8 | Verbs: *be* Verbs + ~*ing*

*be*動詞（どうし）＋動詞（どうし）＋*ing* は『今（いま）～しています』という表現（ひょうげん）だったね。覚（おぼ）えてるかな？

【例（れい）】

I **am washing** my hands.

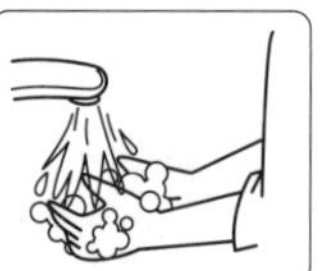

（わたしは今（いま）、手（て）をあらっています。）

He **is playing** soccer.

（かれは今（いま）、サッカーをしています。）

They **are jumping** on the bed.

（かれらは今（いま）、ベットの上（うえ）でジャンプしています。）

Read the sentences. (文（ぶん）を読（よ）んでみよう！)

① 

I am listening to music.

（わたしは今（いま）、音楽（おんがく）をきいています。）

② 

I am reading a book.

（わたしは今（いま）、本（ほん）を読（よ）んでいます。）

③ 

I am looking at a picture.

（わたしは今（いま）、絵（え）を見（よ）ています。）

Say it! Read the sentences.
(文を読んでみよう!)

Grammar2・3で出てきたよ!覚えてるかな?
What are you doing?
(今、何してるの?)
I am walking.
(わたしは今、歩いています。)

Trace the letters and read the sentences.
(点線の文字をなぞって「今〜している」文をよんでみよう!)

① 
I am drinking milk.
(わたしは今、ミルクをのんでいます。)

② I am playing the piano.
(わたしは今、ピアノをひいています。)

③ 
I am picking strawberries.
(わたしは今、いちごをつんでいます。)

④ 
I am eating curry.
(わたしは今、カレーを食べています。)

Let's read the sentences and see how they are different.
（2つの文を読んで、ちがいを見つけよう！）

① You walk every day.（あなたは毎日あるきます。）

You are walking.（あなたは今、あるいています。）

② He plays soccer every day.（彼は毎日サッカーをします。）

He is playing soccer.（彼は今、サッカーをしています。）

③ She cooks every day.（彼女は毎日料理をします。）

She is cooking.（彼女は今、料理をしています。）

④ It runs every day.（それは毎日走ります。）

It is running.（それは今、走っています。）

⑤ We draw pictures every day.（わたしはちは毎日絵を描きます。）

We are drawing pictures.（わたしはちは今、絵を描いています。）

『動詞 ＋ *ing*』にした時、動詞の形がかわるもの

Trace the letters and read the sentences.
（点線の文字をなぞってから文を読んでみよう！）

ルール　動詞の最後に『 e 』がつく単語は『 e 』をとって『 ing 』をつける

① write → writ~~e~~ing

I am writ~~e~~ing a letter.

② make → mak~~e~~ing

We are mak~~e~~ing a cake.

ルール　動詞の最後の文字が重なる

① run + n + ing → running

You are running in the park.

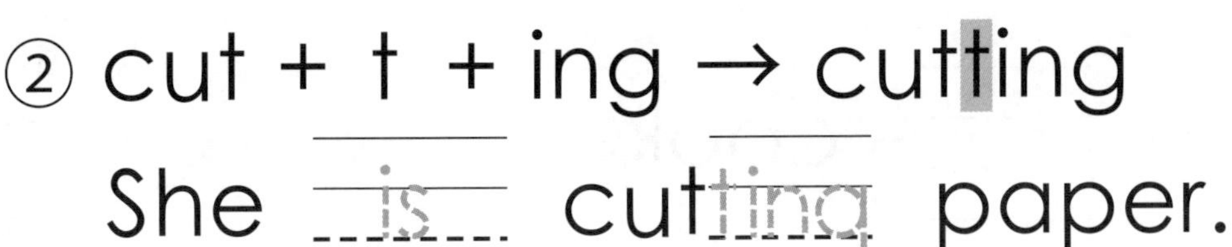

② cut + t + ing → cutting

She is cutting paper.

Complete the sentences.（＿＿ に合うことばを入れて文を完成させよう！）

①  He is pushing the ball.

②  She ＿＿＿ touch＿＿＿ the wall.

③  You ＿＿＿ open＿＿＿ the curtains.

④  It ＿＿＿ sleep＿＿＿.

⑤  They ＿＿＿ play＿＿＿ soccer.

⑥  I ＿＿＿ cook＿＿＿.

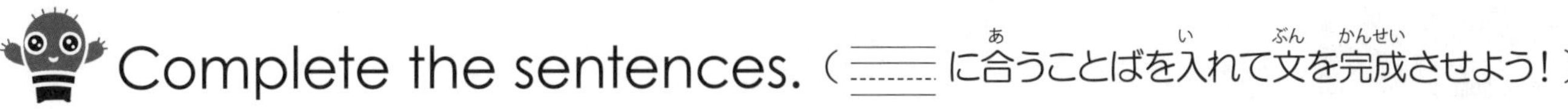

Complete the sentences.（＿＿に合うことばを入れて文を完成させよう！）

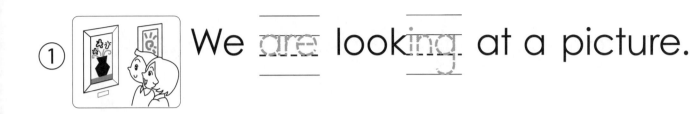

① We are looking at a picture.

② I ______ climb______ a tree.

③ You ______ jump______ on the bed.

④ She ______ putt______ a cup on the table.

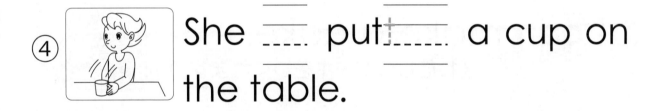

⑤ They ______ com~~e~~______ to school.

⑥ You ______ runn______ in the park.

Section 6 Grammar 2, 3 Review 9 Can

『できる』という意味の『can』は、動きを表わすことばと仲良しで出てくるよ！

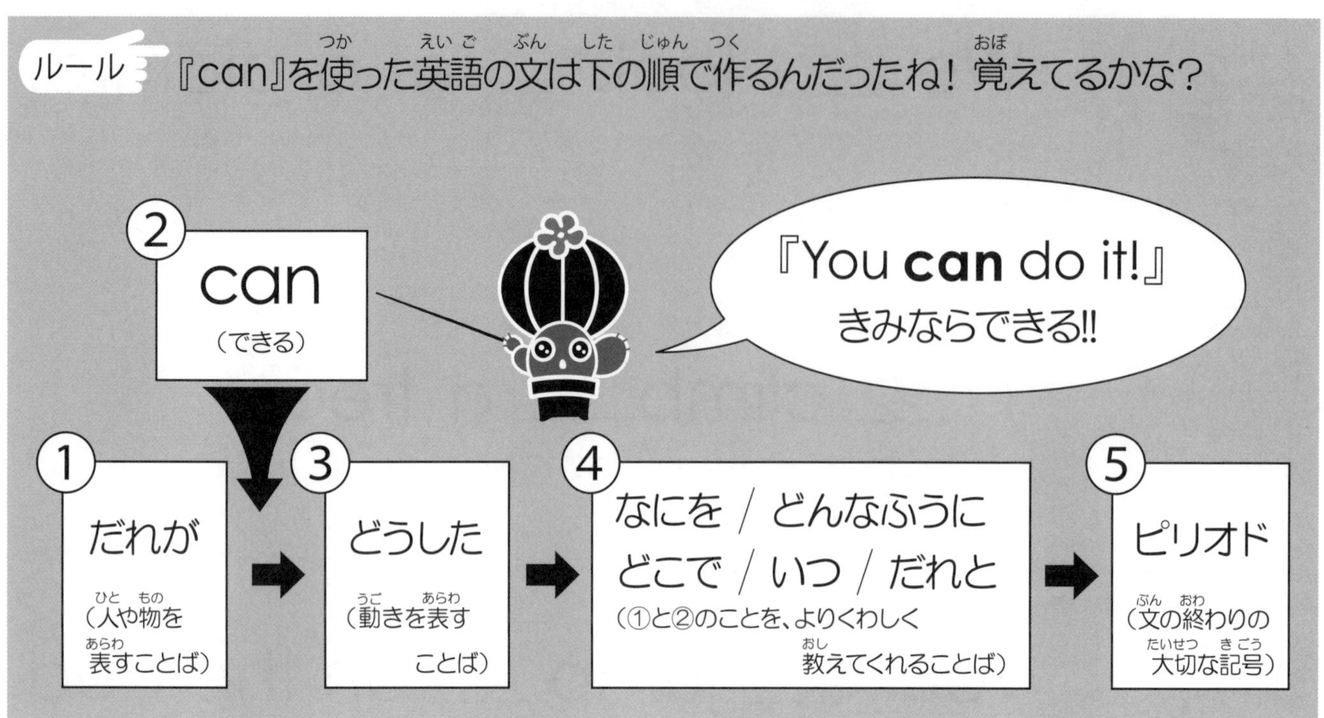

ルール
『can』を使った英語の文は下の順で作るんだったね！覚えてるかな？
② can （できる）
『You can do it!』
きみならできる!!
① だれが （人や物を表すことば）
③ どうした （動きを表すことば）
④ なにを / どんなふうに どこで / いつ / だれと （①と②のことを、よりくわしく教えてくれることば）
⑤ ピリオド （文の終わりの大切な記号）

Let's read the sentences.（文を読んでみよう！）

① I **can** make a cake.
（わたしはケーキをつくれます。）

② I **can** play the piano.
（わたしはピアノをひけます。）

③ I **can** climb a tree.
（ぼくは木にのぼれます。）

④ I **can** run fast.
（わたしははやく走れます。）

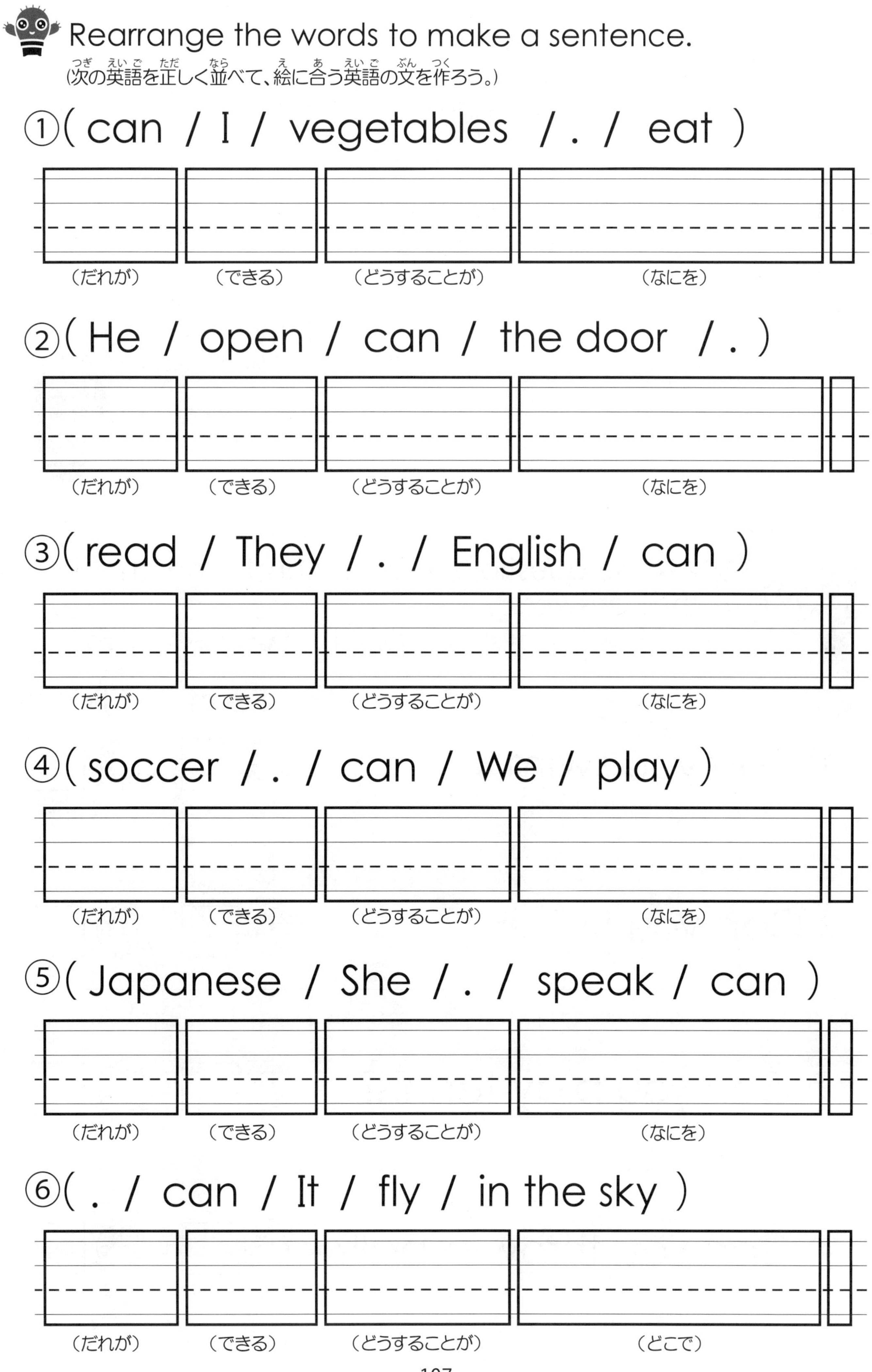

Rearrange the words to make a sentence.

(次の英語を正しく並べて、絵に合う英語の文を作ろう。)

①(can / I / vegetables / . / eat)

(だれが) (できる) (どうすることが) (なにを)

②(He / open / can / the door / .)

(だれが) (できる) (どうすることが) (なにを)

③(read / They / . / English / can)

(だれが) (できる) (どうすることが) (なにを)

④(soccer / . / can / We / play)

(だれが) (できる) (どうすることが) (なにを)

⑤(Japanese / She / . / speak / can)

(だれが) (できる) (どうすることが) (なにを)

⑥(. / can / It / fly / in the sky)

(だれが) (できる) (どうすることが) (どこで)

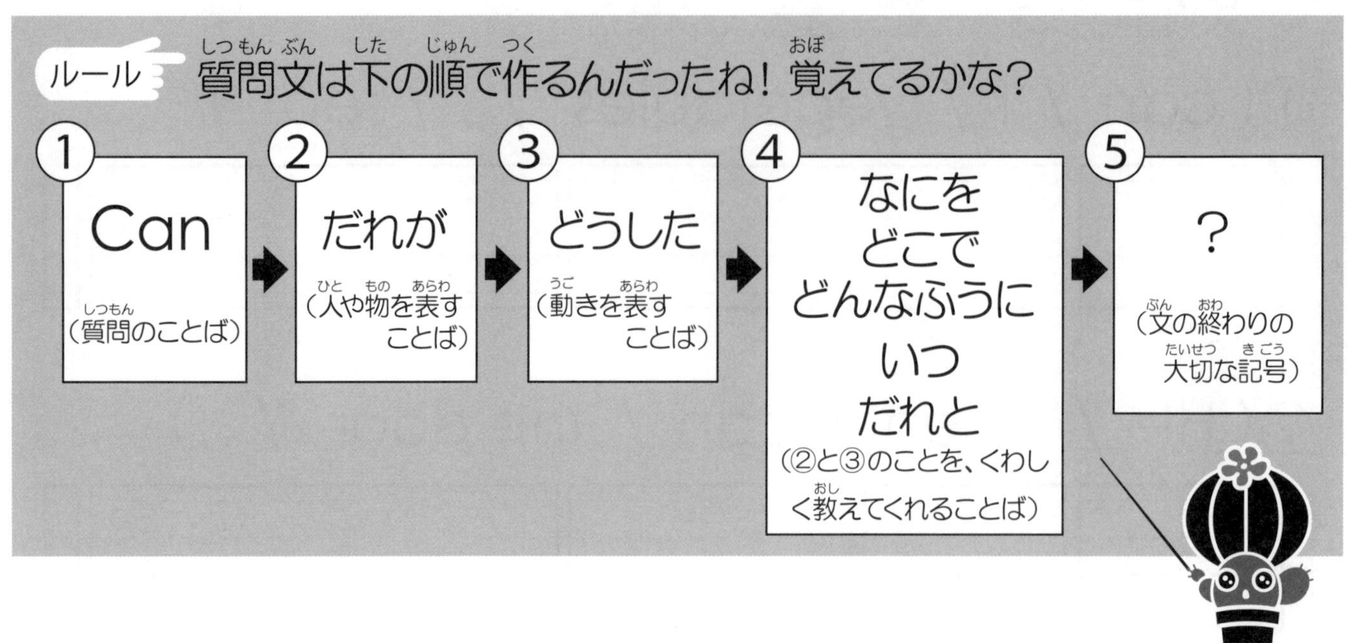
ルール
質問文は下の順で作るんだったね！ 覚えてるかな？
① Can （質問のことば）
② だれが （人や物を表すことば）
③ どうした （動きを表すことば）
④ なにを どこで どんなふうに いつ だれと （②と③のことを、くわしく教えてくれることば）
⑤ ？ （文の終わりの大切な記号）

Say it!

Ask the questions to your friends and check their answers.
（お友達に聞いてみよう！ お友達の答えの方の□に✔（チェック）をしよう！）

Yes, I can. No, I can't.

① Can you swim?

② Can you fly?

③ Can you play tennis?

④ Can you throw a ball?

Make your own questions and ask your friends.
You can use the words from the [ ].
（自分で文をつくってお友達に聞いてみよう！ [ ] の中のことばをつかえるよ！）

Yes, I can. No, I can't.

① Can you ________________ ? ☐ ☐

② Can you ________________ ? ☐ ☐

③ Can you ________________ ? ☐ ☐

④ Can you ________________ ? ☐ ☐

⑤ Can you ________________ ? ☐ ☐

sleep / drink / eat / swim / cook
sing / read / catch / run / climb
fly / write / throw / play

Rearrange the words to make a question.

(（　）の言葉(ことば)を並(なら)べかえて＿＿に正(ただ)しい文(ぶん)を作(つく)ろう！)

①(Can / I / vegetables / ? / eat)

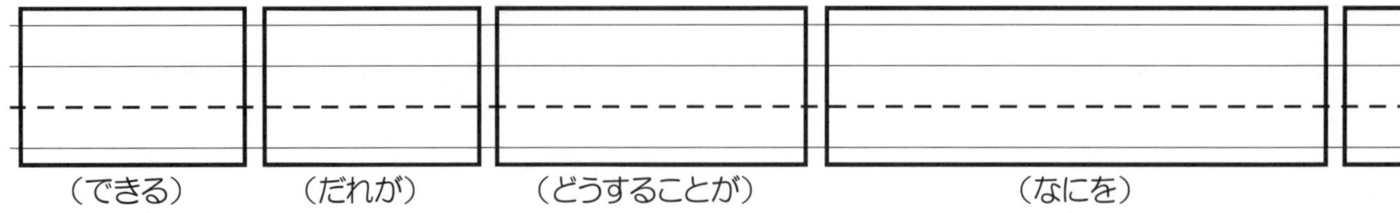

②(he / open / ? / Can / the door)

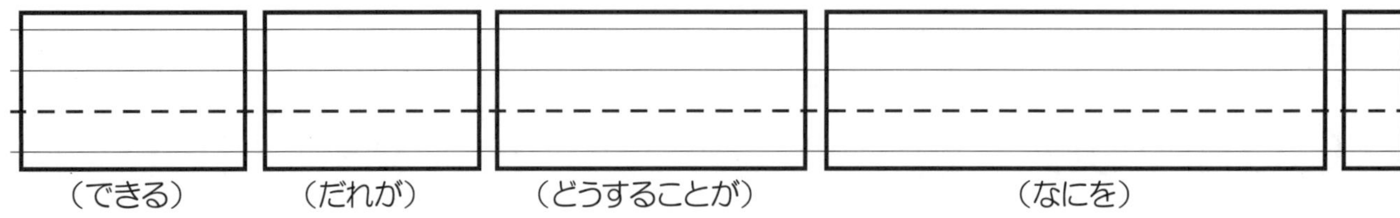

③(read / they / ? / English / Can)

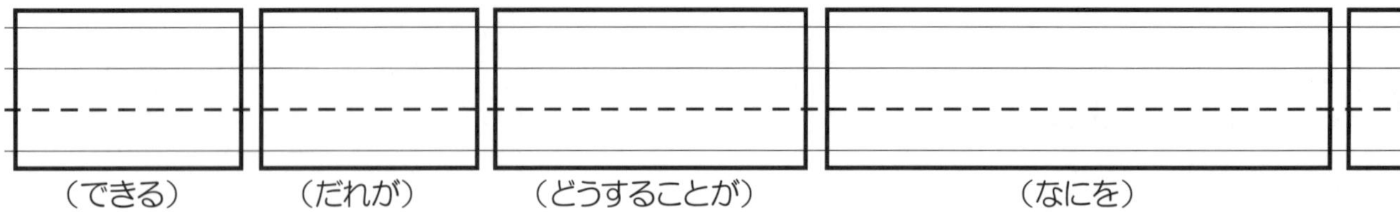

④(soccer / ? / Can / we / play)

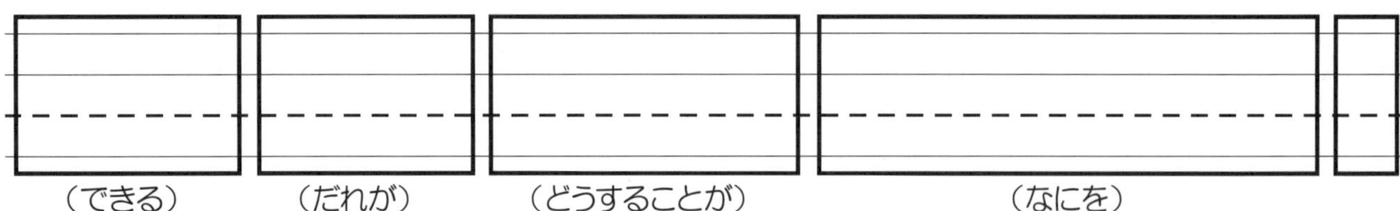

⑤(Japanese / she / ? / speak / Can)

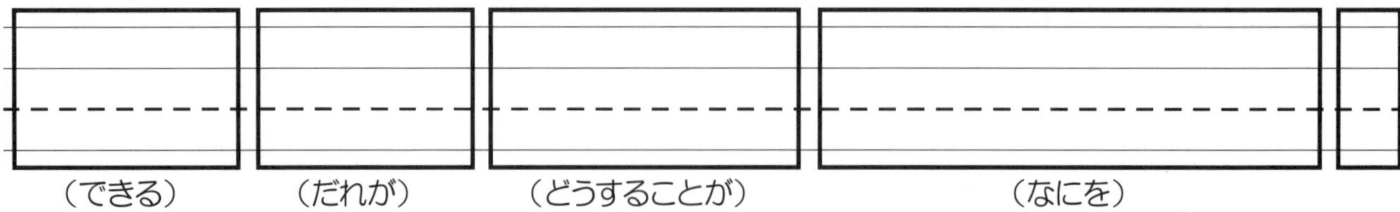

⑥(Can / it / fly / ? / in the sky)

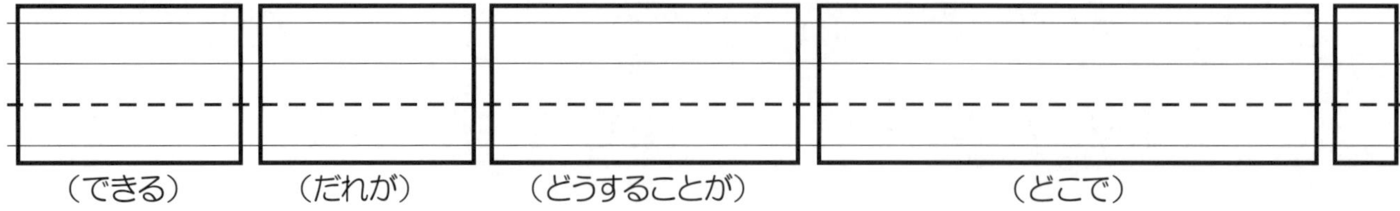

Complete the sentences.（ に合うことばを入れて文を完成させよう！）

① Can she ride a bike?

Yes, she can.

② Can they play soccer?

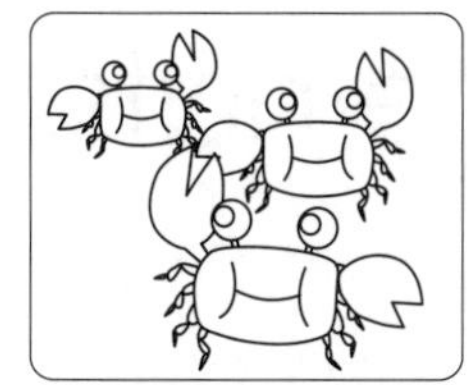

No, they can't.

③ Can he drink milk?

Yes, he can.

④ Can it fly?

No, it can't.

⑤ Can you make a necklace?

Yes, I can.

Section 7 Basic Prepositions

その１『ばしょ』をあらわすことば

P112~116は
Grammar 2, 3の
復習だよ！

Choose the correct word and write it on the lines.
(正しい言葉を下から選んで ____ の上に書こう！)

①The rabbit is ____________ the hat.

②The rabbit is ____________ the hats.

③The rabbit is ____________ the hat.

④The rabbit is ____________ the hat.

⑤The rabbit is ____________ the hat.

⑥The rabbit is ____________ the hat.

in / under / between
on / in front of / by

①The cat is ______________ the bag.

②The girl is ______________ the door.

③The boy is ______________ the tent.

④The turtle is ______________ the box.

⑤The hospital is ______________ the house.

⑥The baskets are ______________ the door

behind / far from / near

Write the correct Japanese on the line.

(「うさぎ」はどこにいる?日本語の線のところに「うさぎ」のいる“ばしょ”を書いてみよう)

Where is the rabbit?
（うさぎはどこにいる?）

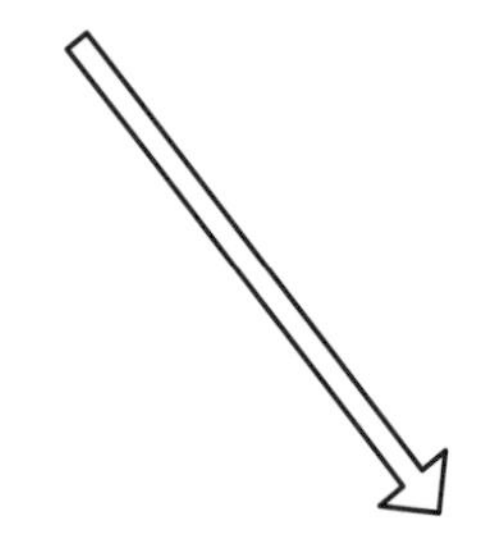

It is by the hat.

うさぎはどこにいる？

⇨ ぼうしの＿＿＿＿＿＿にいます。

It is next to the hat.

うさぎはどこにいる？

⇨ ぼうしの＿＿＿＿＿＿にいます。

It is beside the hat.

うさぎはどこにいる？

⇨ ぼうしの＿＿＿＿＿＿にいます。

みんな意味は似ているよ！

by→そば / next to→となり / beside→となり

Trace the words and write the correct Japanese on the line.
（＿＿の英語をなぞって文を完成させよう！ 英文と意味が合うように、日本語の文の＿＿にも合う言葉を書こう！）

① Where are the pears?

They are next to the fridge.

（ナシは冷蔵庫の＿＿＿＿＿＿です。）

② Where is the camera?

It is by the computer.

（カメラはコンピューターの＿＿＿＿＿＿です。）

③ Where is the hospital?

It is beside the station.

（病院は駅の＿＿＿＿＿＿です。）

Look at the map and answer the questions by writing the correct words on the lines. （地図を見て問題に答えてみよう！答えの文の ＿＿ に当てはまる英語を書いてみよう！）

① What is next to the supermarket?

The ________________ is next to the supermarket.

② What is by the park?

The ________________ is by the park.

③ What is beside the hospital?

The ________________ is beside the hospital.

ルール **in・on・at** は、場所を表わすこともできるけど『時間』を表わすことばの前にも使われるよ！
そして『**～に**』となるんだ。

下の英語を読んでみよう！

in 年・月・季節・午前中・午後などの前につくよ！

【例】
in 1998 （1998年**に**）
in May （5月**に**）
in the summer （夏**に**）
in the morning （午前中**に**）
in the afternoon （午後**に**）

on 曜日・日付などの前につくよ！

【例】
on July 2nd （7月2日**に**）
on Saturday （土曜日**に**）

at 時間などの前につくよ！

【例】
at seven （7時**に**）
at night （夜**に**）

日本語ではどの場合も同じ『**～に**』だけど、
英語では『**in・on・at**』と違うね。
上の文をセットで覚えてしまうといいよ！

Choose the correct word and write it on the lines.
(正しい言葉を下から選んで ______ の上に書こう！)

①See you __________ Friday!

②I get up __________ seven every morning.

③Julia's birthday is __________ August.

④What do you do __________ Christmas Day?

⑤I play with my friend __________ the afternoon.

⑥He watches TV __________ night.

in / on / at

Circle the correct words. (正しいことばに ◯ をつけよう。)

① He goes to school (on / in / at) eight every day.

② Christmas Day is (on / in / at) December 25th.

③ I see stars (on / in / at) night.

④ George and I met (on / in / at) 2014.

⑤ We often go to the beach (on / in / at) the summer.

⑥ Let's meet (on / in / at) 7 p.m. tomorrow.

⑦ Did you go out (on / in / at) Thursday?

⑧ She moved to China (on / in / at) May.

⑨ She takes a piano lesson (on / in / at) Sundays.

Match the pictures to the English sentences.

（絵にあった英語の文を選んで線で結ぼう！）

①  •		• It is cloudy.
②  •		• It is cold.
③  •		• I am full.
④  •		• It is sunny.
⑤  •		• I am hungry.
⑥  •		• It is hot.
⑦  •		• It is windy.
⑧  •		• It is rainy.

Match the pictures to the English sentences.

（絵にあった英語の文を選んで線で結ぼう！）

① •

② •

③ •

④  •

⑤ 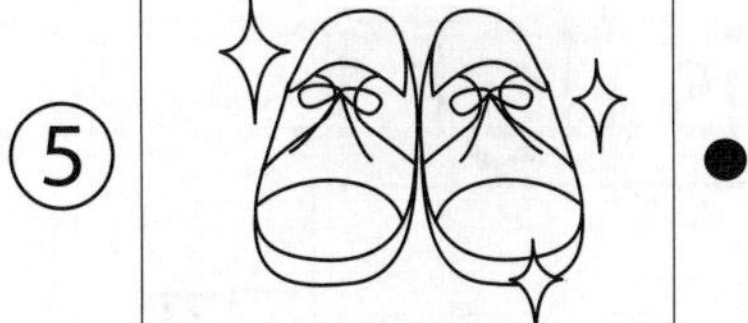 •

⑥  •

⑦  •

⑧  •

• He is tall.

• They are clean.

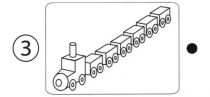

• He is short.

• It is small.

• They are dirty.

• It is big.

• It is long.

• It is short.

Write the correct Japanese in the □.

（　　のことばは人(ひと)や物(もの)の“ようす”を表(あら)わすことばだよ。どんな“ようす”なのか□の中(なか)に日本語(にほんご)で書(か)いてみよう！）

①

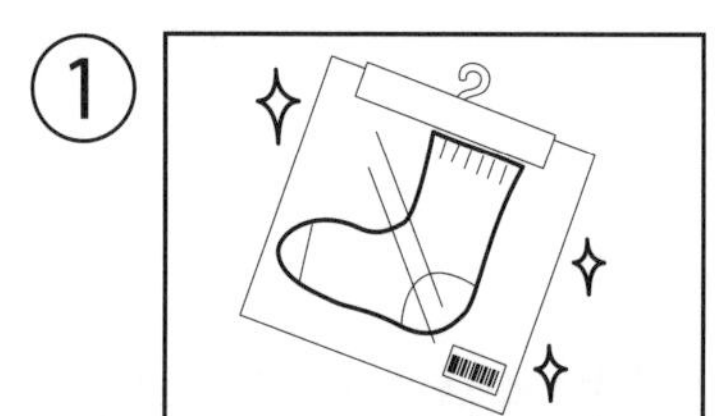

It is **new**.

それは□です。

②

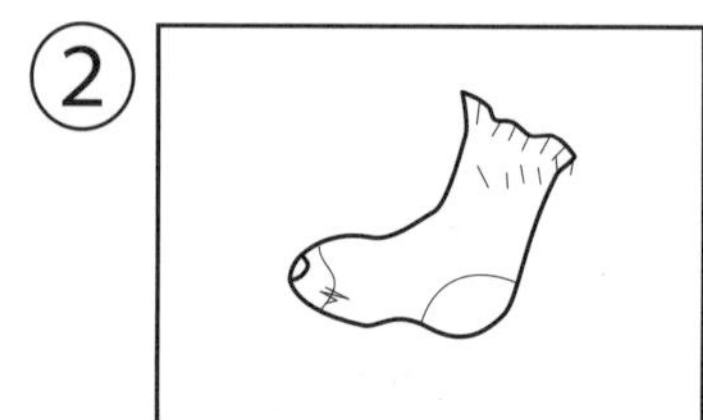

It is **old**.

それは□です。

③

It is **left**.

それは□です。

④

It is **right**.

それは□です。

⑤

It is **fast**.

それは□です。

⑥

It is **slow**.

それは□です。

Write the correct Japanese in the □.

（　のことばは人や物の“ようす”を表わすことばだよ。どんな“ようす”なのか □ の中に日本語で書いてみよう！）

①

It is **good**.

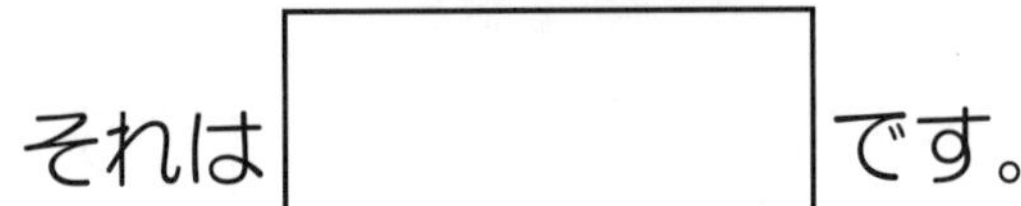

②

It is **bad**.

それは □ です。

③

I am **sad**.

④

I am **happy**.

わたしは □ です。

⑤

It is **thick**.

⑥

It is **thin**.

それは □ です。

Write the correct Japanese in the ☐.

（▭のことばは人や物の“ようす”を表わすことばだよ。
どんな“ようす”なのか☐の中に日本語で書いてみよう！）

Grammar 4
からの新しい言葉だよ！
覚えてね！

①

It is **full**.

それは ______ です。

②
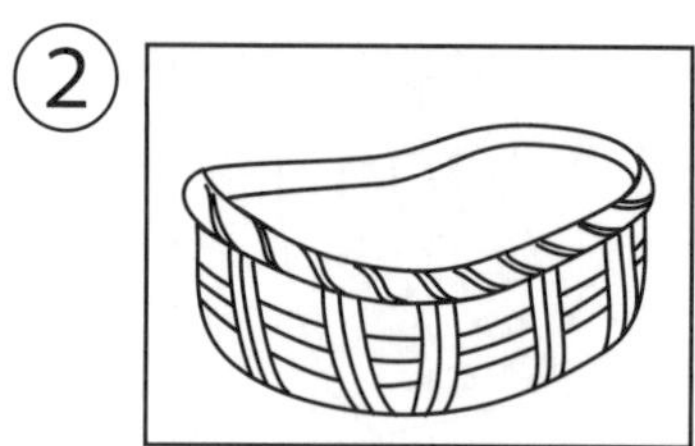

It is **empty**.

それは ______ です。

③

1 + 1 = 2

It is **easy**.

それは ______ です。

④

$\frac{\sqrt{6}}{2}\times(4-y)^2=x$

It is **difficult**.

それは ______ です。

⑤

She is **rich**.

彼女は ______ です。

⑥

She is **poor**.

彼女は ______ です。

Write the correct Japanese in the [ ].

（　のことばは人や物の"ようす"を表わすことばだよ。
どんな"ようす"なのか [ ] の中に日本語で書いてみよう！）

①

It is pretty.

それは [ ] です。

②

It is ugly.

それは [ ] です。

③

They are expensive.

それらは [ ] です。

④

They are cheap.

それらは [ ] です。

⑤

It is early in the morning.

朝 [ ] です。

⑥

It is late at night.

夜 [ ] です。

Say it! Choose the correct word from the ▢ and write it on the lines. Then read the sentences.

（絵を見て、それが「どんな」様子か ▢ から選び線の上に書いてみよう！
それから英文を読んでみよう！）

① I am ______________.

② It is ______________.

③ I am ______________.

④ It is ______________.

⑤ It is ______________.

⑥ They are ______________.

⑦ She is ______________.

big / long / short / windy
cold / new / hungry

Say it!

Choose the correct word from the [ ] and write it on the lines. Then read the sentences.

（絵を見て、それが「どんな」様子か [ ] から選び線の上に書いてみよう！それから英文を読んでみよう！）

① I am ____________.

② He is ____________.

③ It is ____________.

④ They are ____________.

⑤ I am ____________.

⑥ It is ____________.

⑦ It is ____________.

rainy / old / happy / tall
cloudy / full / sunny

Say it! Choose the correct word from the ▢ and write it on the lines. Then read the sentences.

（絵を見て、それが「どんな」様子か ▢ から選び線の上に書いてみよう！
それから英文を読んでみよう！）

① It is his ______________ hand.

② 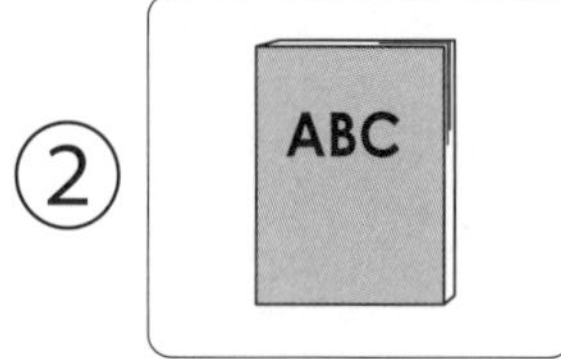

It is ______________.

③ 

It is ______________.

④ 

It is ______________.

⑤ 

They are ______________.

⑥ 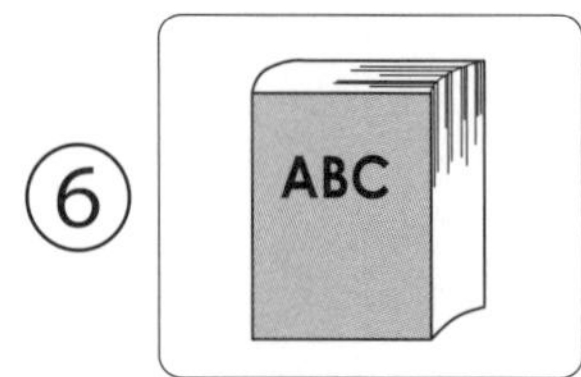

It is ______________.

⑦ 

I am ______________.

fast / sad / short / thin

hot / thick / left

Say it! Choose the correct word from the [ ] and write it on the lines. Then read the sentences.

（絵を見て、それが「どんな」様子か[ ]から選び線の上に書いてみよう！
それから英文を読んでみよう！）

① It is ______.

② It is ______.

③ It is his ______ hand.

④ They are ______.

⑤ They are ______.

⑥ It is ______.

⑦ They are ______.

good / slow / clean / right
dirty / small / bad

Say it!

Choose the correct word from the [box] and write it on the lines. Then read the sentences.

（絵を見て、それが「どんな」様子か [box] から選び線の上に書いてみよう！
それから英文を読んでみよう！）

① They are ______________________.

②  It is ______________________.

③  She is ______________________.

④  She is ______________________.

⑤ 

This homework is ______________________.

⑥ 

This test is ______________________.

expensive / rich / poor
difficult / easy / pretty

Say it! Choose the correct word from the ▢ and write it on the lines. Then read the sentences.

（絵を見て、それが「どんな」様子か ▢ から選び線の上に書いてみよう！
それから英文を読んでみよう！）

① I get up ________________ in the morning.

② 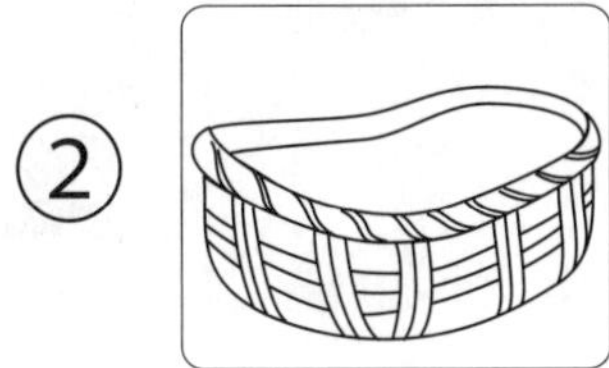

The basket is ________________.

③ 

It is ________________.

④ 

They are ________________.

⑤ 

The basket is ________________.

⑥ 

It is ________________ at night.

cheap / full / late
early / empty / ugly

Section 9　Grammar 4 Review

過去形の復習をしよう

確認！

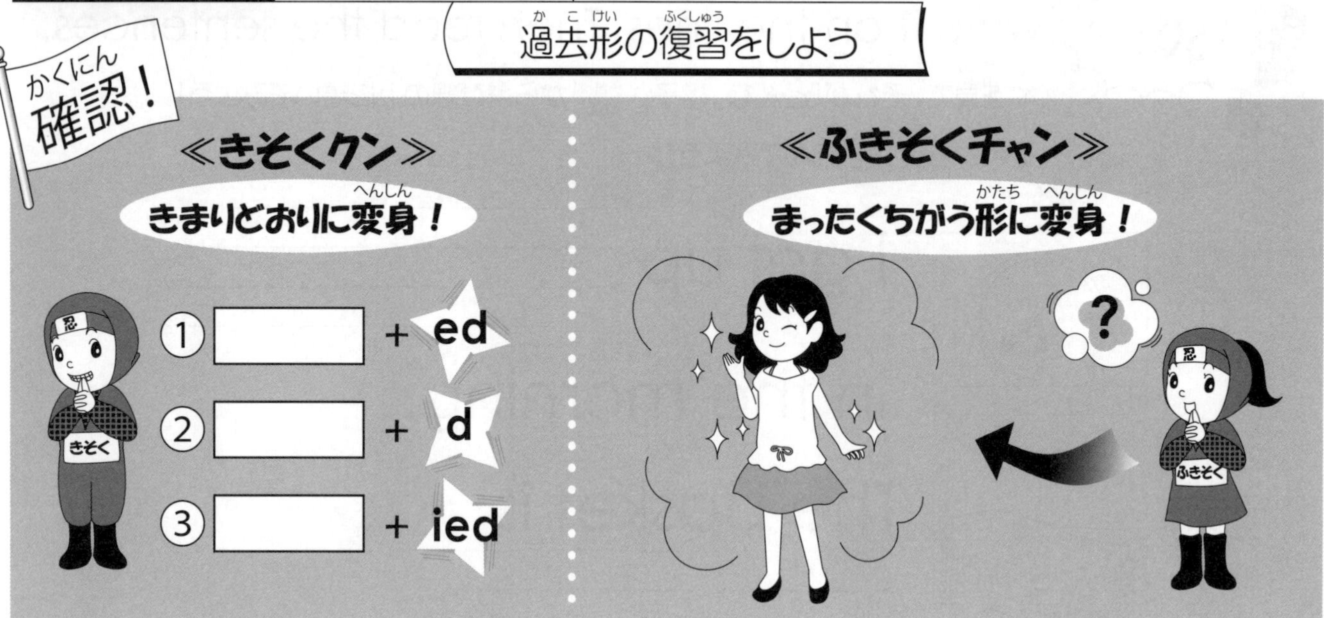

Which group do the words belong to?
Write the correct letter in the (　　).
(下の言葉は次のどっちのグループかな？「**A**」か「**B**」を選んで(　　)に入れよう。)

≪きそくクングループ…**A**　ふきそくチャングループ…**B**≫

go (　　)	cook (　　)
watch (　　)	eat (　　)
have (　　)	help (　　)
open (　　)	close (　　)
see (　　)	get (　　)
live (　　)	study (　　)
come (　　)	write (　　)

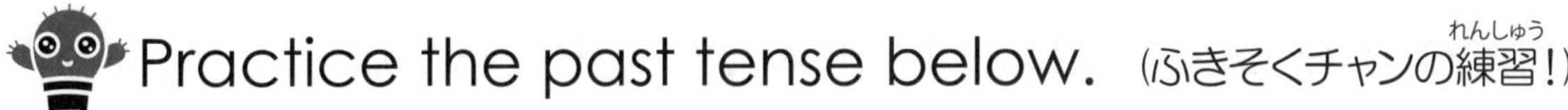

Practice the past tense below. (ふきそくチャンの練習(れんしゅう)!)

(begin → began)

① began

(bring → brought)

② brought

(feel → felt)

③ felt

(find → found)

④ found

(forget → forgot)

⑤ forgot

(know → knew)

⑥ knew

(lose → lost)

⑦ lost

Practice the past tense below. (ふきそくチャンの練習!)

(meet → met)

① met

(say → said)

② said

(see → saw)

③ saw

(think → thought)

④ thought

(take → took)

⑤ took

(tell → told)

⑥ told

苦手な単語を練習しよう!

Practice the past tense below. (きそくクンの練習(れんしゅう)!)

(clean → cleaned)

① cleaned

(finish → finished)

② finished

(show → showed)

③ showed

(talk → talked)

④ talked

(wait → waited)

⑤ waited

Special Review

苦手(にがて)な単語(たんご)を練習(れんしゅう)しよう!

Can you find all the past tense forms of these verbs in the word worm?

(次の中から過去形に変身した言葉を探せるかな?)

csibegantsfeltymsaidingfoundxzsawputtalkedaibthoughtlcleanedorlmetcuwknewterbroughtkutwaitedtookmsshowedtherlostnicforgotletfinishedvittolpdy

①	begin	✓
②	clean	
③	feel	
④	meet	
⑤	say	
⑥	know	
⑦	see	
⑧	talk	
⑨	think	
⑩	find	
⑪	bring	
⑫	finish	
⑬	lose	
⑭	forget	
⑮	take	
⑯	show	
⑰	wait	
⑱	tell	

Fill in the letters and complete the past tense verbs.
(次の__に文字を入れて過去形をつくろう!)

① tell → t _ _ d

② clean → c l _ _ n _ d

③ lose → _ _ s t

④ meet → _ _ t

⑤ take → t _ _ k

⑥ show → s h _ _ _ d

⑦ feel → f _ _ t

⑧ begin → b e g _ n

⑨ think → _ _ o _ g h t

⑩ wait → w _ _ t _ d

⑪ talk → _ a l _ _ d

⑫ see → s _ w

⑬ bring → b _ o u _ _ t

⑭ finish → f _ n _ s h _ d

⑮ know → k _ _ w

⑯ find → f _ u n _

⑰ say → s _ _ d

⑱ forget → f o r g _ t

Special Review

Write the past tense in the ☐.
(次(つぎ)の☐に過去形(かこけい)を書(か)こう!)

① begin →
② forget →
③ clean →
④ know →
⑤ tell →
⑥ think →
⑦ write →
⑧ show →
⑨ meet →
⑩ finish →
⑪ talk →
⑫ see →
⑬ bring →
⑭ feel →
⑮ lose →
⑯ find →
⑰ take →
⑱ say →

Special Review

① わたしは物語(ものがたり)を伝(つた)えた。

a story.

② わたしたちはあなたに地図(ちず)を見(み)せた。

a map to you.

③ かれはかさを教室(きょうしつ)に持(も)ってきた。

an umbrella to the classroom.

④ かれらはうれしく感(かん)じた。

happy.

⑤ かの女(じょ)は消(け)しゴムを見(み)つけた。

an eraser.

⑥ ぼくは宿題(しゅくだい)がおわった。

my homework.

⑦ あなたはわたしの友(とも)だちに会(あ)った。

my friend.

⑧ かの女(じょ)は順番(じゅんばん)を待(ま)った。

for her turn.